Shadow in the Land

Homosexuality in America

Congressman William Dannemeyer

Shadow in the Land

Homosexuality in America

IGNATIUS PRESS   SAN FRANCISCO

Cover by Riz Boncan Marsella

© Ignatius Press, San Francisco, 1989
0–89870–241–0
Library of Congress catalogue number 89–80470
Printed in the United States of America

CONTENTS

Introduction

Before I talk about what's happening in America today, I would like to describe for you the way life used to be in this country before things changed so profoundly in the 1960s. If you are under thirty, you'll probably think the world I'm describing is hopelessly naive and idealized, a time that never existed. But if you're over fifty, you'll know that everything I say is perfectly true.

In the first place, thirty years ago no one questioned the idea that the traditional family was the cornerstone of American society and essential to its very survival. Let me hasten to say that by "traditional family" I mean a man and a woman, married to each other, who have children together and rear them in a community full of other such families. There are some people today who use the word "family" to mean something else entirely—domestic arrangements that have never been termed "familial" in the long history of the West. But a "family" thirty years ago meant Mom, Dad, the kids—and, on holidays, Grandpa, Grandma, aunts, cousins, and in-laws.

In those days, a man and a woman didn't just move into an apartment and live together. Oh, occasionally they did, but the practice was not common, and in small towns it almost never happened. It's easy enough to argue that people were narrow-minded then, but I don't really think they were. I believe they simply saw more clearly the importance of traditional family life to the survival of society as a whole. They recognized that promiscuous conduct threatened the very existence of family life, which allowed young people to grow up among those who loved them, cared for them, and saw that they joined the community at large with some regard for the rights and feelings of others. Those are lessons that you learn best in a family, and if you don't learn them there, sometimes you don't learn them at all.

One of the reasons it was easier to put sexuality in its proper perspective was that the media weren't hawking sex all day long. Hollywood films had to pass very strict industry standards before they were released. You couldn't depict promiscuous conduct as exciting and normative. Americans wouldn't have tolerated such an unhealthy message in those days, and the movie industry understood that attitude. As a matter of fact, Hollywood stars who chose to lead irregular sex lives were careful to keep their activities a secret from their fans.

Playboy and *Penthouse* were just beginning to publish, but they were somewhat different magazines from what they are today; and so-called adult bookstores, currently so obvious in every American city, were virtually unknown. Pornography was considered an affront to public decency and was banned in virtually every community. I know if anyone had set up a porn shop in our neighborhood, he would have been out of business by sundown and would have spent the night in jail. And from that time on he would have been ostracized from respectable society, not because he was a sinner (everybody was a sinner) but because his particular sin undermined the very foundations of society.

In such a world, then, how were homosexuals regarded? Were they, like the pornographer, thrown into jail, ostracized, run out of town? Were they the object of systematic persecution and physical abuse, as some people today say they were? The question is a little more complicated than the National Gay and Lesbian Task Force would have you believe, and I want to take a moment to answer it because it is important that everyone understand several key distinctions the homosexual activists have sought to obscure.

First, no one thirty years ago thought a lot about homosexuality. It was not a topic that preoccupied the average American. You didn't hear it discussed on talk shows or depicted in movies. You didn't see so-called gay pride parades in our

major cities. You weren't bombarded with political pronouncements on the subject. You didn't have homosexuals
militantly proclaiming to the general public the propriety of
what they did in the bedroom. Certainly prominent political
figures did not announce to the world that they habitually
committed homosexual acts and were proud of it.

If someone engaged in such acts, he kept the matter to himself, not only because there were laws against homosexual
conduct but also because the community at large disapproved
of it as much as it disapproved of any kind of abnormal sexual
behavior. Yet people did not regard the homosexual in quite
the same way they regarded the pornographer. Under ordinary circumstances they tolerated him (or her) in their midst,
allowing him to hold a job, move in social circles, and within
limits do whatever he chose with his private life.

Most people over fifty will tell you that they remember few
if any arrests of homosexuals on charges growing out of their
activities, despite the fact that sodomy was illegal in every state
in the Union. Of course, one of the reasons why there were
fewer prosecutions was because there were fewer homosexuals. As I will demonstrate later, homosexuality is not undeni-
ably an inherited "orientation", but is probably a bad habit
acquired in early childhood or puberty. I didn't make up this
explanation; it is the considered opinion of a significant body
of experts in the field, despite what you may have read in the
popular press. Thus, in an age where homosexuality was not
publicly advertised (like soap or chewing gum), relatively few
young people fell into such unnatural behavior. So there
weren't as many practicing homosexuals in society, and hence
there were far fewer arrests than one might have expected,
despite the almost universal legal prohibitions.

But there was another good reason why homosexuals were
not often arrested: they were discreet in their behavior. I don't
mean merely that they didn't carry placards advertising their
homosexuality, as they do today. I mean that, like heterosexuals, they kept their sex lives private—and in so doing paid a

relatively small debt to society for the privilege of doing what they wanted behind closed doors. Indeed, that was all society really asked of them — the right not to be affronted by militant immorality or perversion.

In fact, it is important to remember that while a man and a woman of approximately the same age could not live together in propriety thirty years ago, a couple of the same age and sex could. Thus the practice of homosexuality was relatively easy in the old days — provided you didn't open the bedroom blinds and leave the lights on. Society may have suspected what went on with the blinds drawn, but it didn't come snooping around in the dark. It required merely an outward conformity to its ancient rules.

Why, then, were there laws?

Probably for three reasons. First, because civil law until recently has been the highest expression of communal morality, not just in matters of life and property but in matters of sexual conduct as well. Sexual behavior has always been covered by law not only in Western society but also in Eastern society. Indeed, there is no society in the history of the world where there were not some rules governing sexual conduct — with the possible exception of Sodom. And in some primitive societies, where sexuality seems to be freer, the penalties for violating those strictures are much severer than in Western societies. So law and sexual prohibitions have always been inextricably interwoven.

A second reason why there were laws prohibiting homosexual conduct was to protect the very young. We have always believed as a people that the sexual abuse of children is one of the greatest of all sins, the deliberate corruption of innocence. Statutory rape laws were instituted to protect females below the age of consent, and there were also laws to protect male children — laws against homosexual conduct as a hedge against the abuse of youngsters by people of the same sex.

A third reason why such laws existed was to protect society against public effrontery, the flaunting of patently immoral conduct. The idea—so out of favor today—was a sound one: if you prohibit this conduct by law, then you won't have to be exposed to it in the public arena, where it can set a bad example for other people, and particularly for the young.

So in an earlier time few homosexuals were arrested—but those who were invariably got into trouble because they were misbehaving with minors or because they were unacceptably public in their behavior. The rest—the ones who went about their lives discreetly—may not have been happy, but they were largely undisturbed by community authorities. It was a sad and precarious existence, to be sure, but it was no worse in most respects than the existence of adulterers and other people who indulged in illicit heterosexual activities.

It's important to realize that this fine balance between moral law and individual freedom was one that had existed throughout the history of our nation and was inherited from our ancestors from Europe, where it had been maintained for centuries. A traditional society is always more intricate than its statute books indicate, and those who tamper with such a delicate mechanism do so at a great risk.

And that's precisely what has happened to our country over the past two decades. Social tinkerers—some of them Justices of the U.S. Supreme Court—have taken our traditional way of dealing with sexuality and have so restructured it that it doesn't work anymore. Suddenly we find ourselves in the midst of a sexual revolution that threatens to tear down the very structure of society itself in an attempt to establish "rights" never before defined or known.

From what source do we derive them the "right to sodomize"? Certainly not from the Constitution of the United States. Even the Supreme Court of the past ten years has not dared to say the states can't pass antisodomy laws, though some of the Justices have so argued. So it is not a "civil right"—that is, a right derived from our government or its Constitution.

Not yet.

Is it, then, one of those "unalienable rights" that the Declaration of Independence speaks of, a right that government has no authority to take away? Can we turn to the Declaration and find a source for the current belief, popular among liberals, that somehow, some way people have a right to practice sexual perversion?

Certainly not. The Declaration says that unalienable rights come from the "Creator", from God, and God cannot be officially appealed to, according to our current court. We have no right to mention Him in our schools, much less invoke His name to settle disputes over domestic policy. None of the organizations chiefly committed to the legalization of homosexuality will ever argue that the "right to sodomize" comes from God.

Instead they will appeal to some vague right they have pulled out of their judicial sleeves and waved in front of an increasingly credulous public. Maybe it will be a "right to privacy", as it was in the case of abortion—a brand new right devised to accommodate the political whims of Justice Blackmun, who can find a right for every prejudice he holds in opposition to the will of decent people. Maybe it will be some new right unknown as yet to the Justice, who even now is trying to dream it up.

Eager to help, some voices in mainline Christian churches have suggested that homosexuality is consonant with Holy Scripture, that the prohibitions in both the Old Testament and the New Testament can be discounted or explained away, that God actually smiles upon homosexual unions, which are just as good and natural as heterosexual unions between married people. Two churches have officially sanctioned curricula that make this argument, and they are teaching these curricula in their church schools, despite the protests of many outraged members. (More about these programs in a later chapter.)

But the fact remains that all of the legal legerdemain and all the theological double-talk cannot legitimize sodomy as a "right" under any existent American political document or philosophical tradition. It remains a persistent scandal in our midst, cherished and revered by a few politicians and the media and promoted by an interlocking directorate of political pressure groups, including the National Gay and Lesbian Task Force, the American Civil Liberties Union, the National Organization of Women, and People for the American Way. It is also a cause close to the heart of the Democratic party. It was no surprise to read in the spring of 1988, when six candidates still remained in the race, that every single aspirant to the Democratic nomination for President had agreed to sign into law a "national gay rights bill" if Congress passed one.

One Republican, George Bush, answered the same questionnaire. Bush said he would veto the bill.

In this respect Bush is one of the few voices in America willing to speak out against the political agenda of this militant bloc of homosexual activists, which increases with each new success. If you want to know just how far these activists have come, consider the following facts:

- The Human Rights Campaign Fund, the homosexual political action committee (PAC), is now the ninth-largest independent PAC in the nation, having moved up from sixteenth the year before. In 1987—not an election year— they were one of only nine PACs out of over 4,000 that spent over $1 million to push their political agenda. They openly boast that they supported more than 100 candidates for the Senate and House in 1986 and have three full-time lobbyists in Washington, D.C.

- The effect of the homosexual movement on federal legislation has been stunning. When those of us who support traditional moral values tried to make it illegal for federal AIDS money to be used to promote homosexuality, they were able to influence the Senate and House conferees to alter the wording of our amendment (which had passed both houses by overwhelming votes), thereby leaving a loophole that rendered the legislation virtually useless.

- Influenced by representatives of homosexual activist groups, a recent Federal Task Force on Youth Suicide tentatively recommended (1) that the Boy Scouts and 4-H Clubs actively seek out homosexual youths and (2) that homosexual scoutmasters and 4-H Club adult leaders also be recruited.

- On October 11, 1987, at least 200,000 homosexual men and lesbians gathered in the nation's capital to demand that their liaisons be recognized by law as equal to those of married heterosexuals. They demanded such things as the right to file joint income tax returns and the right to adopt children. During this rally one speaker proclaimed that 12 percent of the children in the country are "our kids", meaning that 12 percent of the children will join their ranks and become homosexuals.

- Homosexual activists have been able to intimidate officials of the public health service to the point that they have developed entirely new medical policies to deal with AIDS. No longer are testing, reporting, and tracing standard procedures in managing this sexually transmitted disease, as has always been the case with gonorrhea and syphilis. In some states a doctor may not even tell a man's wife that her husband is infected, despite the fact that her life may be endangered by the withholding of such information. These things have been done because homosexuals have complained that without such alterations in traditional practice, they will be exposed to harassment.

- In a deliberately planned campaign of intimidation, a group of homosexuals stormed the annual meeting of the American Psychiatric Association (APA) and through the use of physical threats and disruptive tactics bullied the frightened delegates into voting on the issue of whether or not to reclassify homosexuality as "normal" rather than as a "mental illness". The more traditional members of the organization appealed the ruling to the membership at large, and the officers of the APA allowed the National Gay and Lesbian Task Force partially to draft and entirely to fund a letter justifying the action and urging the members to support it. Later one admirer of this blitzkrieg wrote a book, boasting about the triumph of their strong-arm tactics.

- Homosexuals have organized a national group called AIDS Coalition to Unleash Power (ACT-UP), whose chief tactic is to attend meetings and events where the AIDS agenda is not to their choosing and either disrupt the discussion or else break it up entirely. ACT-UP is more than an application on a widespread level of the tactics used against the American Psychiatric Association. These tactics are a deliberate denial of freedom of speech and freedom of assembly to those organizations and people who might provide an intelligent opposition to ACT-UP's political agenda.

- Homosexuals are now insisting that young people be taught how to perform homosexual acts as well as heterosexual acts. They demand that such instruction be mandatory in our public schools and that the courses also teach that homosexuality is a normal and desirable appetite. Many schools have instituted such sex education.

- In fact, the homosexuals are proclaiming that they will no longer be satisfied with mere acceptance by our society. They are now demanding official approbation. One book is pointedly entitled *The Homosexualization of America*, and in their newspapers and magazines homosexuals openly proclaim their intention to destroy traditional American society —our families, our churches, our deepest religious beliefs.

How are we, as supporters of the Judeo-Christian ethic, supposed to respond to this well-planned and well-financed attack on our civilization? The question faces us wherever we turn, demanding an answer—not in ten years, not in two years, but this year, now! Already we have allowed the tactics of the militant homosexuals to confuse us with appeals to our sense of fairness, with false scientific data, with litigation in courts at every level, and with threats against the public order—all simultaneously. And instead of responding as a united people, we have either surrendered at the outset or else responded in one of several inappropriate ways.

1. We have tried to ignore the phenomenon in hopes that it will go away. It won't. We must either defeat militant homosexuality or it will defeat us. These people have made it clear: they will give us no third choice.

2. We have resorted to name-calling and ridicule, confirming in the eyes of fair-minded people that we are as hardhearted and contemptuous as the National Gay and Lesbian Task Force says we are. In taking this tactic, we deny the humanity of other children of God and forfeit our right to speak as the true keepers of the Judeo-Christian heritage.

3. We have attempted to compromise our principles, reaffirming our opposition to homosexual conduct while arguing that under the American Constitution we have no right to forbid them much of what they want. Such tactics fail to recognize the essential soundness of our Constitution and its foundations in a religious vision of life. We do not have to concede a single point to these people, so long as we retain our sense of charity and our capacity to love even those who want to pervert our society.

What, then, is our proper course of action in the immediate future? How can we completely subdue this malevolent force and at the same time retain our own humanity? In short, how can we remain a nation that affirms the family as the foundation of our civilization?

I will attempt to answer these questions in the pages that follow. These answers will not be simple, nor will the course of action I recommend be easy. Yet I am convinced that once the American people understand the complexities of the issue, they will have the courage to do what is necessary, despite the burden of responsibility they will have to assume.

We must not allow our children to be the victims of an unnatural appetite that has become obsessive in our society. There are specific things we must do in order to prevent this from happening. But first we must understand who we are opposing and on what legal and moral ground we stand. And it is with those questions that I will begin.

CHAPTER ONE

What Really Causes Homosexuality?

In recent years a number of organized homosexual groups and the press have been saying that the question of homosexual origins has been finally and definitively answered, that the results from the latest studies are conclusive. No longer will people be able to argue, as they've done in the past, that homosexuals choose to commit deviant acts or even that homosexuality is a personality disorder brought about by environmental circumstances. It is now certain: homosexuality is genetically determined or else the result of hormonal factors. No two ways about it.

Such is the impression we have from newspaper accounts, from television discussion programs, and from the men and women who speak for the organized homosexual movement. No one, however, seems willing to subject these assumptions to careful scrutiny. They are usually referred to in a sentence or two, as if they were based on accepted laws of modern social science.

Such is not the case.

In the first place, there is no such thing as a "law" in the social sciences. Indeed, there is no such thing as a universally accepted opinion, not on any issue that matters. Social science is as much a part of the humanities as it is of the sciences, and the best sociologists and psychologists use intuitive insight as often as they use the scientific method to reach conclusions. That's why psychologists are always changing their minds about what goes on in the human psyche and why sociologists disagree over what factors are most important in our culture.

That is also why social scientists have always disagreed on what causes a homosexual to behave as he does, and why there will never be unanimity on the subject.

Then, too, this particular controversy has more riding on it than a disagreement over whether or not only children are more likely to become compulsive eaters in later life. The homosexual movement in America is perhaps the most well organized and most disciplined pressure group in the country today. They have carefully planned their moves over the last decade, and their success has been greater than even they might have expected. For example, by 1987 their political action committee, the Human Rights Campaign Fund, was the sixteenth-largest independent PAC in the nation, and by 1988 they were number nine. They have cultivated the media, tirelessly repeating their own version of reality in their own invented language. First the press accepted the word *gay;* then they accepted *homophobia.* Small wonder that they would accept the matter-of-fact statement that no longer was it scientifically respectable to believe that homosexuality was a personality flaw or an illness.

As a congressman who must vote on bills relevant to problems such as AIDS and "gay rights", I have not had the luxury of accepting the popular account of homosexuality, as the reporters have. I have had to examine the assumptions that underlie much of this proposed legislation in order to make reasonable decisions. The nation is faced with the gravest epidemic in modern times. Homosexual conduct has been the prime cause of this plague in our society. The reason the homosexual community has been so devastated is because so many homosexuals are extremely promiscuous, as many studies indicate (e.g., Bell and Weinberg in *Homosexualities*).[1] So I have had to read the scientific literature in order to cast my vote intelligently in behalf of my constituents.

One of the first things I did was write to members of the Committee on Gay, Lesbian, and Bisexual Issues of the American Psychiatric Association (APA), an organization that in 1973 altered its *Diagnostic and Statistical Manual of Mental Dis-*

---

[1] Alan P. Bell and Martin S. Weinberg, *Homosexualities* (New York: 1978).

orders to remove homosexuality from the list of mental illnesses. I wrote to the five members of that committee in order to determine why this action had been taken. Two of the five failed to respond to my inquiry. A third, while affirming his support for the 1973 decision, hid behind an apron of semantics and refused to respond to my request, claiming he didn't understand what I meant by "normal" and "abnormal".

However, the two remaining members responded, and for the first time I began to get some sense of what went on in the APA. The first letter, from Dr. Terry Stein of Michigan State University, was lengthy and detailed. Dr. Stein told me that he had been President of the Association of Gay and Lesbian Psychiatrists and active in a number of organizations and groups studying these issues. He compared earlier attitudes toward homosexuality with racism, suggested that both were products of ignorance, and then offered a brief history of how the APA reached its decision in 1973. He summarized current opinion by saying that no new studies had been published since 1973 that contradicted the conclusions of the APA.

The second full response was from Dr. Robert Paul Cabaj of Brookline, Massachusetts, who lists himself as Deputy Representative of Homosexually Identified Psychiatrists of the American Psychiatric Association. Like Dr. Stein, Dr. Cabaj spent much of his letter talking about the "prejudice and bias" of the past. His categorical pronouncement: people are born with their sexual orientation.

He concluded by urging me to write to Dr. Stein, calling him one of the most learned members of the committee.

Had I accepted these opinions as fact—and clearly many reporters have—then I would have stopped my research and joined the chorus of the uninformed. However, I made further inquiries; and with the help of an excellent staff, I found out just how wrong Dr. Stein was in saying no one had "contradicted" the APA since 1973.

As a matter of fact, there are a number of psychoanalysts who contradict the official APA position in the year 1989;

according to some, those who believe that homosexuality is a pathology may still be in the majority. How, then, can members of the Committee on Gay, Lesbian, and Bisexual Issues so boldly claim unanimity in the field? The short answer to the question is: "They can't." The long answer is an involved narrative.

I. The Storming of the APA

The story of how homosexuality was declared "normal" by the American Psychiatric Association is one of the most depressing narratives in the annals of modern medicine. Indeed, it is difficult to contemplate the details without wondering if our society is not in a state of advanced deterioration. In brief, a group of homosexuals stormed the APA annual convention on successive years and with deliberately disruptive tactics actually forced the psychiatrists to accede to their demands and declare homosexuality a "normal condition". In effect the nature of medical opinion was altered by strong-arm tactics.

This is not an event you will see memorialized on "60 Minutes" or in the *New York Times*. The liberal press is silent on the subject, because, although they are embarrassed by what happened, they are pleased enough by the outcome. Thus have they condoned this politicalization of the medical profession, this defiance of the very idea of thoughtful deliberation and civilized discourse.

A few of the people who were victimized by this unprecedented activity have written on the subject, but perhaps the most detailed account of what happened is to be found in Ronald Bayer's remarkable book *Homosexuality and American Psychiatry: The Politics of Diagnosis* (pp. 101-54).

I say "remarkable" because Bayer's study is a highly sympathetic narrative of these events, yet one that looks unblinkingly at the violence and irrationality that lie at the heart of the homosexual movement, its essentially anarchic impulse. If you doubt that homosexuality should have remained on the list of mental illnesses, you have only to read the account of how it was removed.

What follows is my own summary of the events, a summary derived in large part from Bayer's narrative.

After describing the growing tendency toward disruption and violence in homosexual activism, Bayer tells us that because the APA convention of 1970 was being held in San Francisco, the homosexual leadership decided to focus a concerted attack on that particular organization. This was principally because the APA's official publication, the *Diagnostic and Statistical Manual of Psychiatric Disorders*, had perennially listed homosexuality as a mental illness. That fact stirred up the homosexuals' "wrath", which was already directed against "psychiatry as a social institution".

So the homosexual leadership planned to engage "in the first systematic effort to disrupt the annual meetings of the American Psychiatric Association". As Bayer puts it, "Guerrilla theater tactics and more straightforward shouting matches characterized their presence."[2]

A panel on "transsexualism and homosexuality" was in progress. Irving Bieber, a well-known authority on the subject, was suddenly challenged by the claque of homosexual activists in the meeting room. Bayer tells us what happened:

> His efforts to explain his position to his challengers were met with derisive laughter. Since the norms of civility were considered mere conventions designed to mute outrage, it was not difficult for a protester to call him a ——. "I've read your book, Dr. Bieber, and if that book talked about black people the way it talks about homosexuals, you'd be drawn and quartered

[2] Ronald Bayer, *Homosexuality and American Psychiatry: The Politics of Diagnosis* (New York: 1981), 102.

and you'd deserve it." This verbal attack with its violent tone caused Bieber considerable distress.[3]

Understandably so! Bieber's opinion was widely held and widely expressed—and it was supported by considerable clinical evidence. To equate racism with standard medical diagnosis was either thoughtless demagoguery or else the manifestation of intellectual and moral confusion.

The Bieber confrontation was not the end of the matter. Later, in a crowded room, an Australian psychiatrist, Nathaniel McConaghy, was discussing the use of "aversive conditioning techniques" in the treatment of sexual deviation when the room exploded with "[s]houts of 'vicious,' 'torture,' and 'Where did you take your residency, Auschwitz?' "[4]

Then the protestors demanded to be heard in rebuttal: "We've listened to you, now you listen to us." When someone tried to quiet them down, they shot back, "We've waited five thousand years." And then one protestor began to read from a list of "gay demands". Someone in the room called the protestor a "maniac" and called his female companion "a paranoid fool" and a "bitch".[5]

Astounding as it may seem, instead of calling the police and having the entire crew of intruders hustled off to jail, those in charge adjourned the meeting. Most of the psychiatrists angrily departed, leaving the homosexuals in possession of the room, where they told the small group of psychiatrists remaining that their profession was, as Bayer put it, "an instrument of oppression and torture". In a sense that scene was in miniature a replica of what would soon happen to the entire psychiatric profession.

One psychiatrist, Dr. Kent Robinson, was particularly impressed by the comparison of the homosexuals' plight to that of Blacks in an earlier era. He met with Larry Littlejohn, one of the leading activists, and "agreed with Littlejohn that

[3] Ibid., 102–3.
[4] Ibid., 103.
[5] Ibid.

the tactics employed at the meeting were necessitated by the Association's systematic refusal to let homosexuals appear on the official program".[6]

Robinson agreed to become the "go-between" and present to the APA the homosexuals' demand that they be allowed to present a panel at the next meeting. Robinson subsequently warned John Ewing, chairman of the Program Committee, that if the homosexuals weren't given what they wanted, the entire 1971 meeting might be in jeopardy: "They're not going to break up just one section."[7]

Bayer describes Ewing's response: "Noting the coercive terms of the request, Ewing quickly agreed, stipulating only that, in accordance with APA convention regulations, a psychiatrist chair the proposed session."[8] Robinson agreed to chair the panel.

But complete surrender wasn't enough for the homosexuals. Again Bayer:

> Despite the agreement to allow homosexuals to conduct their own panel discussion at the 1971 convention, gay activists in Washington felt that they had to provide yet another jolt to the psychiatric profession. Accepting a limited role in the program without engaging in a more direct attack on psychiatry might have slowed the momentum necessary to force a retreat on the central issue, the classification of homosexuality as a mental disease. Too smooth a transition toward the institutionalization of protest would have deprived the movement of its most important weapon—the threat of disorder. Aware of the organizational weakness of his own Mattachine Society as well as of its relative conservatism, Frank Kameny turned to a Gay Liberation Front collective in Washington to plan the May 1971 demonstration. Together with the collective, Kameny developed a detailed strategy for disruption, paying attention to the most intricate logistical details, including the floor plan of the hotel in which the convention was to be housed.[9]

[6] Ibid., 103–4.
[7] Ibid., 104.
[8] Ibid.
[9] Ibid., 104–5.

Aware that they might experience some disruption, officials of the APA hired a "special security consultant . . . to map a strategy for diffusing potentially explosive confrontations". In addition to the homosexuals, the officials were worried about a huge antiwar demonstration that was scheduled in Washington at the same time as the APA convention. But apparently the officials were oblivious to how radical the plans of the homosexuals were because, as Bayer put it: "In an effort to limit the extent of possible violence, the APA's leaders decided to avoid, at all cost, any reliance upon a show of force by uniformed guards or police."[10]

They might well have wished for the entire Washington force when, on May 3, a horde of homosexuals and antiwar activists broke into the Convocation of Fellows and destroyed whatever hopes the psychiatrists had concerning a peaceful and orderly discussion of homosexual problems. Kameny grabbed the microphone and told the psychiatrists they had no right even to discuss the subject of homosexuality: "Psychiatry is the enemy incarnate", he declaimed. "Psychiatry has waged a relentless war of extermination against us. You may take this as a declaration of war against you."[11]

From that moment forward the convention was dominated by intimidation, invective, and growing chaos. Bayer reports that the homesexuals' plan to silence opposing medical opinion even extended to the literature being distributed at the convention:

> Using forged credentials, gay activists gained access to the exhibit area and, coming across a display marketing aversive conditioning techniques for the treatment of homosexuals, demanded its removal. Threats were made against the exhibitor, who was told that unless his booth was dismantled, it would be torn down. After frantic behind-the-scenes consulta-

---

[10] Ibid., 105.
[11] Ibid.

tions, and in an effort to avoid violence, the convention leadership agreed to have the booth removed.[12]

When Kent Robinson, who was still mediating between the homosexuals and the psychiatrists, tried to protest the nature and intensity of these activities, he was told that his protests would not be heeded. In the presentation that followed, a five-member panel of "gay activists" delivered a highly emotional defense of their "life-style" coupled with teeth-grinding denunciations of psychiatry and psychiatrists. "We're rejecting you all as our owners. We possess ourselves and we speak for ourselves and we will take care of our own destinies", Kameny said, and a lesbian, Del Martin, said that "psychiatry was the most dangerous enemy of homosexuals in contemporary society".[13]

None of the psychiatrists present dared to raise a voice in protest against the homosexuals' arguments or their conduct. At the end of the convention, emboldened by the success of what they had done thus far, the homosexual activists demanded to appear before the Association's Committee on Nomenclature. Their request was duly received, though not acted on, and, as Bayer put it, "[t]he process of transforming general outrage into a specific *political* demand had been set in motion"[14] (emphasis added).

By 1972 the homosexuals were "a fully institutionalized . . . presence at the annual meeting". They even had Falk Foundation support to come to the convention and to set up a booth where they could deliver their literature. This time the mood was one of half-appeased petulance rather than anger. A flier by Frank Kameny offered the APA peace—at a price:

We are trying to open dialogue with the psychiatric profession. . . . In past years it has been necessary, on occasion, to resort to strong measures against a resisting profession in order to achieve such discussion of *our* problems *with* us instead

[12] Ibid., 105–6.
[13] Ibid., 106.
[14] Ibid., 107.

of merely about us. We sincerely hope that resolution, constructive discussion and dialogue followed by meaningful reform of psychiatry will soon proceed[15] [emphasis in original].

Then came the olive branch, accompanied by an implicit threat:

> Our themes are: Gay, Proud and Healthy and Gay is Good. With or without you we will work vigorously toward [their acceptance]; and will fight those who oppose us. We would much prefer to work with you than against you. Will you join us, to our mutual benefit?[16]

The homosexuals' "second annual panel" consisted of Kameny; Barbara Gittings, a lesbian activist; and three members who were, in fact, professionally qualified to speak: Robert Seidenberg, a psychiatrist from Upstate Medical Center in Syracuse; Judd Marmor, a well-known medical apologist for homosexuals; and Dr. Anonymous, cloaked, masked, and a homosexual psychiatrist.

The burden of their argument was what classical logicians called *argumentum ad misericordiam:* a fallacious form of reasoning that appeals to pity rather than to the merits of the issue at hand. (After all, the question of whether or not homosexuals were mentally ill was a separate issue from whether or not a particular psychiatrist suffered humiliation as the result of that diagnosis.)

Dr. Anonymous, who may well have been no doctor at all, said the following:

> As psychiatrists who are homosexual, we must know our place and what we must do to be successful. If our goal is high academic achievement, a level of earning capacity equal to our fellows, or admission to a psychiatric institute, we must make sure that we behave ourselves and that no one in a position of power is aware of our sexual preference and/or gender identity. Much like a black man with white skin who chooses to live as a white man, we can't be seen with our real friends, our real homosexual

[15] Ibid., 108.
[16] Ibid.

family, lest our secret be known and our doom sealed. . . .
Those who are willing to speak out openly will do so only if
they have little to lose, and if you have little to lose, you won't
be listened to.[17]

It seems hardly necessary to point out that the same argument could be made by a child molester or a gang rapist; yet
Dr. Anonymous' presentation was followed by Seidenberg's
similar appeal, in which he said: "As charitable as I can possibly be towards my own discipline and profession, I cannot . . .
say that psychiatry or psychoanalysis is a friend of the
homosexual."[18]

Marmor predictably echoed this sentiment: "The cruelty,
the thoughtlessness, the lack of common humanity, in the attitudes reflected by many conservative psychiatrists is I think a
disgrace to our profession."[19] In his spirit of thoughtful charity
he singled out one man for special vilification, saying that
Charles Socarides had written a "monstrous attack" on homosexuality. Socarides was for years Marmor's chief scholarly
rival and a man whose reputation for sympathetic treatment of
homosexual patients was widely known.

It is distressing to relate that not a single person raised a
voice to refute this line of reasoning. As Bayer pointed out:

Frank Kameny noted with discernible pleasure that for this first
time at these meetings the only views on homosexuality heard in
public forums were those that could be considered friendly [i.e.,
that homosexuality was "normal"]. . . .
    In accounting for the willingness of the APA to tolerate a
panel so blatantly critical of psychiatric practice and theory, Barbara Gittings commented that it would have taken decades for
such an event to occur "if gay people had politely waited to be
asked." The tactical reliance upon disruption and force in earlier
years had been vindicated.[20]

[17] Ibid., 110.
[18] Ibid.
[19] Ibid., 111.
[20] Ibid.

And indeed it had! Within twenty-four months the American Psychiatric Association had completely surrendered its integrity and self-determination to the homosexual activists. The homosexuals had demanded and received an unprecedented "preferred status" in the profession. They had gained this advantage only because they had violated all the rules, written and unwritten, of formal medical discourse. If you want to know when the ultimate politicizing of American health care occurred, you need look no further than these three meetings and the one that followed.

The proof of the homosexuals' newfound power lay in whether or not they could force the entire psychiatric profession to change its official opinion on the nature of homosexuality—and to do so as the result of physical intimidation and emotional appeals to unreflective pity.

After 1971, in the wake of the invasion of the APA, some of the prominent leaders in the psychiatric establishment were ready to cave in. Henry Brill, who chaired the all-important Nomenclature Committee, wrote that his committee was perhaps willing to acknowledge that homosexual behavior was not necessarily a sign of psychiatric disorder: and that the diagnostic manual should reflect that understanding. [21]

Predictably, in 1973 the homosexuals got their panel, which by then had become de rigueur. Perhaps just as predictably, they were awarded their hearing before the Nomenclature Committee, which was held on February 8. Their case was presented by Charles Silverstein of the Institute for Human Identity, which Bayer describes as "a homosexual and bisexual counseling center". [22]

Silverstein, mustering the authorities who sided with him—and there were some (e.g., Seymour Halleck, Wardell Pomeroy, Alan Bell, Evelyn Hooker, Richard Green, Martin Hoffman, and Judd Marmor)—made a presentation in which he insisted that the vast literature on the other side of the

[21] Ibid., 113.
[22] Ibid., 117.

argument consisted of "scientific errors", and once again he relied heavily on *argumentum ad misericordiam:*

> We are told, from the time we first recognize our homosexual feelings, that our love for other human beings is sick, childish and subject to "cure." We are told that we are emotional cripples forever condemned to an emotional status below that of the "whole" people who run the world. The result of this in many cases is to contribute to a self-image that often lowers the sights we set for ourselves in life, and many of us asked ourselves, "How could anybody love me?" or "How can I love somebody who must be just as sick as I am?"[23]

Silverstein undoubtedly knew what Bayer acknowledges in his account, that "none of the committee members was an expert on homosexuality". Therefore he presented his "scientific evidence" as conclusive:

> I suppose what we're saying is that you must choose between the undocumented theories that have unjustly harmed a great number of people and continue to harm them and . . . controlled scientific studies. . . . It is no sin to have made an error in the past, but surely you will mock the principles of scientific research upon which the diagnostic system is based if you turn your backs on the only objective evidence we have.[24]

Such a simplistic and biased statement of the argument should have been met with a fair measure of skepticism, but the Nomenclature Committee, without bothering to listen to the other side, indicated that they would favorably consider the redefinition of homosexuality. This decision was clearly the result of severe intimidation followed by what appeared to be sweet reasonableness—a variation of the bad-cop/good-cop method of intimidating reluctant witnesses into full confessions.

But the homosexuals weren't through with the committee. In order to make certain that they weren't influenced by "con-

[23] Ibid., 119.
[24] Ibid., 119–20.

servative professional tendencies", the homosexuals gave the
story to the *New York Times*, which over the years has been a
chief conduit of homosexual medical propaganda. Bayer
believes that this strategy paid off: "With the reevaluation of
the status of homosexuality a matter of public record, Brill
reported that he hoped to present a statement on the appropriate direction of change within four months, in time for the
May 1973 APA convention."[25]

According to Bayer, that statement was initially framed by
Robert Spitzer, a member of the Nomenclature Committee
who, in wrestling with his own changing attitudes, came up
with a position that accommodated the demands to take
homosexuality off the list of mental illnesses while at the same
time leaving the psychoanalysts with something of their position intact. In so doing, Spitzer chose to redefine the meaning
of "mental disorder". In order for something to be classified as
a "mental disorder", it would have to be accompanied by
"subjective distress" or "some generalized impairment in
social effectiveness or functioning". Homosexuality did not
always fit this description. Therefore, homosexuality would
henceforth be called "a form of irregular sexual development",
and anyone who was having mental problems as a result of
homosexuality would be said to be suffering from "sexual orientation disturbance"—a "psychiatric disorder".

It was this concept that Spitzer brought before the Nomenclature Committee, careful to point out that he was not saying
homosexuality was "normal", since he himself regarded it as
"less than optimal". His statement had something for everybody, and it seemed that he had solved the problem of what to
do about the militant homosexuals. He even drafted a statement on the civil rights of homosexuals that passed the
Nomenclature Committee unanimously. This statement
called for a more tolerant and compassionate treatment of
homosexuals and the repeal of all laws forbidding homosexual

[25] Ibid., 121.

behavior between consenting adults. Then the entire package was sent along to the Council on Research and Development.

But the homosexuals were not satisfied. Ronald Gold of the National Gay Task Force wrote to the council attacking Spitzer's proposal on the grounds that it was discriminatory against homosexuals, since it assumed that they would be the only ones worried about their sexual orientation. Heterosexuals might also need help in changing their sexual orientation to become homosexuals. Besides, this kind of statement would allow "indiscriminate attempts" by psychiatrists to change the orientation of homosexuals "suffering from the internalized effects of antihomosexual bigotry".

Bayer also describes Gold's attack on Spitzer:

> The Spitzer paper was criticized not only because it did not embrace the view that homosexuality was a normal variant of human sexuality, but also because of its emphasis on the extent to which homosexuality was "suboptimal." Referring to Spitzer's comparisons of homosexuality, religious fanaticism, and racism as "egregious," Gold asserted that the paper's discussion of "valuable" and "optimal" behavior was unscientific, revealing an attitude that ought to be irrelevant to psychiatry and the diagnosis of disorders.[26]

Such an attack—directed at a man who had reinvented the manual for homosexuals—indicated either supreme confidence or else borderline madness. It is a wonder that Spitzer didn't withdraw in sullen fury. Yet he persisted in his support of his proposal, and eventually it passed the Council on Research and Development and later the trustees of the APA.

At this meeting Charles Socarides, Irving Bieber, and Robert McDevitt—who, unlike the other psychiatrists involved in this controversy, were experts on the subject of homosexuality—were permitted to give an opposing viewpoint, though Bayer makes it clear that the result was already a foregone conclusion. Socarides would later write that after all the months of

---

[26] Ibid., 131.

homosexual lobbying and testimony, he and his two colleagues were given only fifteen minutes for their rebuttal.

The homosexuals and their friends at the APA held a joint
press conference at which they called for the repeal of all laws
prohibiting consensual sexual relations between adults of the
same sex. The next day headlines told the news all over the
country: "Doctors Rule Homosexuals Not Abnormal".

Believing that the process by which this change came about
was tainted, Socarides, Bieber, and others decided to appeal
the ruling to the membership at large, thereby providing for a
referendum on the decision. Though the officers of the APA
bristled at the idea, they finally decided to allow the vote, realizing that too much controversy already surrounded their
decision.

However, Socarides and his supporters were no match for
the homosexuals, who were old hands at conducting direct-
mail campaigns. They contacted their old ally Kent Robinson,
who in turn contacted Judd Marmor, at that time a candidate
for the presidency of the APA. What did the homosexuals
want? A statement, signed by Marmor and others, that would
discredit the Socarides group and influence fellow psychiatrists
to support the decision of the board of trustees. Eventually
Marmor, his opponents in the presidential race, and two current vice-presidents agreed to sign the statement, which was
written by Robert Spitzer and by Ronald Gold of the National
Gay Task Force, and which in part read as follows:

> The undersigned recognize the complexity of the many issues
> involved in this decision and the diversity of views within our
> Association. Nonetheless, we feel that it would be a serious and
> potentially embarrassing step for our profession to vote down a
> decision which was taken after serious and extended consider-
> ation by the bodies within our organization designated to con-
> sider such matters. We therefore urge you to vote to retain the
> nomenclature change.[27]

[27] Ibid., 145.

Not only did the homosexual activists promote the idea and help draft the letter; they also bought the APA mailing list and sent out the letters to the membership. In order to pay for this substantial direct-mail campaign, the National Gay Task Force sent out a fund-raising appeal to their membership.

Bayer drops into the passive voice in explaining why the participants chose not to reveal the collusion involved in this ploy:

> Though the NGTF played a central role in this effort, a decision was made not to indicate on the letter that it was written, at least in part, by the Gay Task Force, nor to reveal that its distribution was funded by contributions the Task Force had raised. Indeed, the letter gave every indication of having been conceived and mailed by those who signed it. What remains in doubt is the extent to which the signers collectively either encouraged or acquiesced in that decision. Though each publicly denied any role in the dissimulation, at least one signer had warned privately that to acknowledge the organizational role of the gay community would have been the "kiss of death."
>
> There is no question, however, about the extent to which the officers of the APA were aware of both the letter's origins and the mechanics of its distribution. They, as well as the National Gay Task Force, understood the letter as performing a vital role in the effort to turn back the challenge.[28]

The result of the referendum was an affirmation of the decision by the trustees, though by no means an overwhelming vote of confidence: 58 percent in favor, 40 percent either against or abstaining. No one knows how much the mailing or the activities of the homosexual community aided in this victory, but their role in the two-year process was crucial and decisive. By a variety of tactics unprecedented in American professional circles, they not only had captured the American Psychiatric Association but also had established a strong presence in the health care community. Shortly thereafter, for example, they easily gained the same kind of policy statement from the American Psychological Association, which in more

[28] Ibid., 146.

recent years has become one of their most aggressive allies in court fights to remove from the books laws that forbid homosexual acts.

As a postscript, I must note that in the latest edition of the *Diagnostic and Statistical Manual (DSM-III)* you will find two alterations from the revisions passed in 1973. First, there is no longer any mention of homosexuality in the manual, because a subsequent battle, in which Spitzer fought on the other side, resulted in the elimination of so-called ego-dystonic homosexuality on the grounds that the reference was discriminatory. Second, pedophilia has undergone a change in description that suggests a new toleration on the part of psychiatrists, one that may bode ill for the future.

If the past is any indication of the future, in the next few years what we have known as "child molesting" will be officially termed a "normal variant of human sexuality", and its practitioners will successfully argue before a quaking group of psychiatrists that *any* mention of it in the *Diagnostic and Statistical Manual* would be cruel and discriminatory.

If this account seems beyond belief or excessively harsh, remember that Ronald Bayer is *sympathetic* with everything the homosexuals did and applauds the ultimate outcome of their activities. He is not the least bit concerned with the manner in which medical opinion was subverted by invective and the threat of irrational force. He mirrors perfectly the homosexuals' preoccupation with their own political ends.

Having read Bayer's disturbing book, I see more clearly the reasons why the medical questions surrounding homosexuality have received so little thoughtful examination, why on the basis of a handful of studies many doctors and many more reporters and politicians say with great haste that homosexuality is inherited and that law, religion, and education must reflect that "incontrovertible fact". We have come to the point in this country where some matters are no longer debatable, even when there are intelligent and decent people on both sides of the question. It is significant, I think, that Bayer cites Herbert Marcuse, the radical Marxist of the 1960s, in justifying the repression of opposing views on the issue of the origins of homosexuality:

> Far more significant, however, was a shift in the role of dem-onstrations from a form of expression to a tactic of disruption. In this regard gay activists mirrored the passage of confrontation politics that had become the cutting edge of radical and antiwar student groups. The purpose of protest was no longer to make public a point of view, but rather to halt unacceptable activities. With ideology seen as an instrument of domination, the tradi-tional willingness to tolerate the views of one's opponents was discarded. Those who sought intellectual justification for this change found it in Herbert Marcuse's essay "Repressive Tolerance."[29]

This statement sums up the nature of the medical debate over homosexuality and, for that matter, over AIDS. Only one side is acceptable, permissible, respectable. If anyone attempts to state an opposing opinion, it is ignored. Better for the public to believe that such opinions don't exist. As for those authorities who can't be ignored, they are savaged, dis-missed as ignorant or bigoted or worse.

II. Contemporary Explanations of Homosexuality

Given the climate in which the debate over homosexuality must be carried on, it is difficult to make sense out of the var-ious theories that are currently abroad. In the first place, there are many different scientific accounts of how men and women come to feel sexual attraction for members of their own sex— but these opinions seem to fall into two basic categories. One deterministic view holds that homosexuality is an inherited predisposition. The other maintains that it is the result of envi-ronmental influences. (Needless to say, scientists have never

[29] Ibid., 98–99.

been interested in a third alternative—i.e., that such matters may involve free will and are therefore too mysterious to deal with in absolute scientific terms.)

There are studies that support both heredity and environment as the absolute determinant of "sexual orientation" or "predisposition". However, it is fair to say that no one has yet produced evidence that other experts, equally as qualified, have not been able to discount. There is considerable debate.

In order to understand the degree to which this question has been distorted through oversimplification, it is necessary to examine the studies of a number of authorities in the field. In so doing, however, I must point out that one cannot merely choose the latest findings, as many commentators have been tempted to do. As the following survey of scholarship will indicate, conclusions have a way of being superseded by later refinements of the same experiment. In order to make this point clear, I have chosen to trace a few of the most frequently cited studies from their first publication to their testing and qualification by later scholars. You can be certain that the latest findings will be subject to the same ruthless refutation.

A. THEORIES THAT VIEW HOMOSEXUALITY AS INHERITED

1. *Genetic Theories*

The genetic explanation of homosexuality is the one that many homosexuals prefer. They argue that if homosexuality is a genetic trait, like color of eyes or hair, then it is not something homosexuals can be held accountable for—and that it is not "unnatural", since genetic traits are the mysterious decrees of nature itself, operating to create a rich variety in life. We all like the idea of different colors of eyes and hair, so why not a third sex? Or a fourth? However, if homosexuality is a perversion of what is natural, then homosexuals must look at their own conduct in an entirely different light and explain it in less satisfying terms.

Also, to say that homosexuals behave as they do because they are born that way helps them in arguing for their political agenda in ways that have been successful in the recent past. For example, they can equate their own position with that of Blacks, who, because of genetic traits, have been deprived of equal protection under the law. Homosexuals argue that they too have suffered from something predetermined before they ever saw the light of day.

What, then, do those studies really tell us?

The study I have seen most frequently cited is F. J. Kallman's "Comparative Twin Study on the Genetic Aspects of Male Homosexuality", [30] first published over thirty-five years ago in 1952. Kallman analyzed the histories of thirty-seven pairs of identical twins (twins who came from one fertilized egg) and twenty-six pairs of fraternal twins (separate eggs fertilized by separate sperm) and reported that in 100 percent of the cases of identical twins where homosexuality occurred, both were homosexual, while in the fraternal twins only in 12 percent of the cases were both homosexual.

On the surface this study seemed to prove a genetic predisposition toward homosexuality, but several subsequent researchers[31] raised serious methodological questions and cast substantial doubts on the Kallman results. In fact, several have cited numerous examples of identical twins where only one is homosexual. [32]

[30] F. J. Kallman, "Comparative Twin Study on the Genetic Aspects of Male Homosexuality", *Journal of Nervous and Mental Disorders* 115 (1952): 283.

[31] For example, D. Rosenthal, *Genetic Theory and Abnormal Behavior* (New York: 1970).

[32] For example, J. D. Rainier, A. Mensikoff, L. C. Kolb, and A. Carr, "Homosexuality and Heterosexuality in Identical Twins", *Psychosomatic Medicine* 22 (1960): 251; G. K. Klintworth, "A Pair of Male Monozygotic Twins Discordant for Homosexuality", *Journal of Nervous and Mental Disorders* 135 (1962): 113; N. Parker, "Twins: A Psychiatric Study of a Neurotic Group", *Medical Journal of Australia* 2 (1964): 735; and L. L. Heston and J. Shields, "Homosexuality in Twins", *Archives of Genetic Psychiatry* 18 (1968): 149.

The Heston and Shields study (see note 32) is particularly interesting since it cites twelve cases of twins diagnosed as homosexual, five of whom were identical twins. In three cases both twins were homosexual, and in two cases only one was homosexual.

What conclusions are we to draw from this evidence? In a comprehensive essay on the question, Anthony Wakeling has written: "No firm conclusion can be drawn from these studies. A higher concordance rate for homosexuality in twins is not necessarily due to genetic factors, but may result from factors such as intense identification or specific environmental practices related to twinships."[33]

Wakeling goes on to admit the possibility that genetic factors may be somehow involved in the way homosexuality has its genesis, perhaps by causing *some* people to be more sensitized to particular environmental influences, among them those that cause homosexuality. In other words, while there is no proof that genetic factors cause anyone to prefer erotic acts with those of their own sex, genes may cause some of them to be particularly vulnerable to the influence of a possessive mother or a cruel and overbearing father, and it is such factors as these that many psychiatrists and psychotherapists believe are responsible for the personality disorder known as homosexuality.

2. *Hormonal Factors at Birth*

People who experiment with animals have theorized in the past two decades that hormones in fetuses, particularly "androgens", play an important role in affecting behavior in adult members of the species. Indeed, some experiments have shown that a deprivation of androgen in a male fetus will cause

---

[33] Anthony Wakeling, "A General Psychiatric Approach to Sexual Deviation", in Ismond Rosen, ed., *Sexual Deviation* (Oxford: 1979), 1–28.

the animal to behave in some respects like a female after it has matured, even though it has fully developed male parts.

These kinds of results have been obtained in studies of rhesus monkeys, and there are some people who would like to draw the same conclusions about human beings. But the behavior of the monkeys (they are less rowdy than the other males) does not necessarily relate to their sexual activities. And while decreasing levels of rough-and-tumble play might affect a male's relationship with both his peers and parents, as R. Green has shown in *Child Psychiatry: Modern Approaches*,[34] no one has yet proven that hormonal deficiencies in human beings result in less aggressive behavior.

Again, even if some connection were established between androgen deficiencies and homosexual behavior, it would not mean that the one caused the other. It might indicate that the more feminine behavior promoted relationships between child and parents or child and playmates that resulted in a homosexual orientation.

3. *Levels of Testosterone*

In 1970, three years before the American Psychiatric Association declared homosexuality a "normal condition", S. Margolese published a study called "Homosexuality: A New Endocrine Correlate."[35] In it he reported that after studying samples of urine, he could demonstrate a clear difference in the levels of testosterone between homosexual and heterosexual males. That same year researchers found similar results in testing two male homosexuals and four female homosexuals: low levels in the males, high levels in the females.[36] And a year

[34] Richard Green, "Atypical Psychosexual Development", in M. Rutter and L. Hersov, eds., *Child Psychiatry: Modern Approaches* (Oxford: 1977).

[35] S. Margolese, "Homosexuality: A New Endocrine Correlate", *Hormonal Behavior* 1 (1970): 151.

[36] J. A. Loraine, A. A. A. Ismail, D. A. Adamopoulas, and G. A. Dove, "Endocrine Function in Male and Female Homosexuals", *British Medical Journal* 4 (1970): 406.

later, in a test measuring the plasma testosterone levels in
thirty homosexual males and a control group of heterosexual
males, researchers reported lower plasma testosterone levels in
the homosexuals.[37] Again it appeared as if hormonal factors
did play some part in the development of homosexual conduct. However, subsequent studies, published around the
time of the American Psychiatric Association decision, failed
to replicate the same findings.[38]

Perhaps even more significant was the report of researchers
who found *higher* levels of testosterone in homosexuals than in
heterosexuals,[39] thereby complicating the picture to the point
where no definitive conclusions could be drawn by an objective investigator.

Why, then, have all of these hormonal and endocrinal studies created such a confused picture? Has someone been deliberately distorting research to prove a point, or have there been
a careless or unscientific collection and evaluation of data? The
answer to both of these questions is probably "no". In the first
place, many of these studies are by physical scientists who are
simply engaged in highly sophisticated measurements. Their
results are not quite so subject to ideological manipulation as
those collected by social scientists.

But more importantly, other factors have to be taken into
consideration in evaluating levels of androgens and testosterone, factors not reflected in a simple division into heterosexual
and homosexual. For example, androgen levels in particular
are affected by both physical and emotional stress.[40] Thus,

[37] R. C. Kolodny, W. H. Masters, J. Hendryx, and G. Toro, "Plasma Testosterone and Semen Analysis in Male Homosexuals", *New England Journal of
Medicine* 285 (1971): 1170.
[38] See G. Tourney and L. M. Hatfield, "Androgen Metabolism in Schizo-
phrenics, Homosexuals, and Controls", *Biological Psychiatry* 6 (1973): 23.
[39] H. K. H. Brodie, N. Gartrell, C. Doering, and T. Rhue, "Plasma Testosterone Levels in Heterosexual and Homosexual Men", *American Journal of
Psychiatry* 131 (1974): 82.
[40] See R. M. Rose, P. G. Bourne, and R. O. Poe, "Androgen Response to
Stress", *Psychosomatic Medicine* 31 (1969): 418.

men who live more stressful lives are more apt to have low androgen levels.

Then, too, sexual activity can play a major role in determining plasma testosterone levels.[41] If a homosexual group, for example, had been more sexually active than a heterosexual control group, then plasma testosterone levels might indeed be lower by virtue of that factor alone. (And it is perhaps relevant to note that most studies on the subject suggest that homosexuals average many more sexual contacts than do heterosexual men.)

Finally, another study[42] clearly suggests the impact of drug usage on hormones. Thus, if homosexuals are greater drug and alcohol users, and some studies suggest they are, then as a group they might show lower testosterone levels.

So one thing is certain: hormonal levels can reflect more than one cause, and it is therefore difficult to say that a consistently low level of androgen or plasma testosterone pre-existed and therefore resulted in homosexual behavior.

Given the conflicting opinions, homosexual activists, picking and choosing from among the many studies, can make a convincing case to those who don't know the scholarship that homosexuality is an inherited "orientation", that it is therefore "natural" and "normal" for some people, and that the laws of the land should be altered to reflect these "facts".

Homosexuals have voiced these opinions so loud and so long that the news media have begun to echo their statements with the same degree of certitude. For many uninformed liberals, it is now a "fact" that homosexuality is hereditary just as it is a "fact" that the moon circles the earth. But even though hard scientific data such as we find in the studies cited above

[41] C. A. Fox, A. A. A. Ismail, D. N. Love, K. E. Kirkham, and J. A. Loraine, "Studies on the Relationship between Plasma Testosterone Levels and Human Sexual Activity", *Journal of Endocrinology* 52 (1972): 51.
[42] R. C. Kolodny, W. H. Masters, R. M. Kolodner, and G. Toro, "Depression of Plasma Testosterone Levels after Chronic Intensive Marijuana Use", *New England Journal of Medicine* 290 (1974): 872.

cannot be as easily manipulated as the data of the social sciences, the world of the physical sciences also has its contradictions and uncertainties, and these must be admitted, even at the expense of having a perfectly manageable world, one that supports all your personal and political prejudices.

I have found that homosexual activists are simply unwilling to acknowledge the complexity of their own sad plight. They want so desperately to believe they are somehow "normal" and "natural" in what they do that they snatch at any theory that seems to support that idea, ignoring the enormous body of opinion among researchers and psychotherapists that tells a different and less satisfying tale.

In order to see the other side of the question, let's examine the statements of a number of psychiatrists and psychologists who, contrary to Dr. Stein's bland assumptions, "contradict" what the APA said and did, remembering that in many cases they are therapists whose careers have been devoted to treating homosexuals and who are therefore familiar with case histories as well as abstract theory. They have no political axes to grind. They are not people who find homosexuality intimidating or personally revolting. Among them you will find a very high level of compassion; otherwise they would not have chosen to specialize in such work.

Yet the story they tell is clearly disturbing to homosexual activists and their political allies.

B. THEORIES THAT VIEW HOMOSEXUALITY
AS ACQUIRED BEHAVIOR

First, apparently a significant proportion of psychiatrists and psychologists actively engaged in treating patients still believe that homosexuality is, in most cases, an abnormal condition and, in some cases, a serious mental disorder. Others in this category believe that it is no more than an alternate way of behaving, like left-handedness. But all reject the idea that homosexual behavior is *inherited* or *instinctual*. Having considered the evidence, pro and con, they maintain that homosexuality is a response to environmental conditions.

Some say that this response is inevitable, that a poor relationship with parents automatically produces a homosexual. Others say that these conditions merely make people more vulnerable, though they too tend to believe that in the histories of all homosexuals such disturbing relationships can be found. Those I cite are joined in this opinion by many other sexologists and researchers.

Among those who state that homosexuality is acquired behavior are the following:

Wainwright Churchill in *Homosexual Behavior among Males:*

There are no sexual instincts in man . . . human sexuality is entirely dependent upon learning and conditioning. The individual's pattern of sexual behavior is *acquired* [emphasis in original] in the context of his unique experiences and [is] in no sense innate or inherited.[43]

Robert Frumkin in *The Encyclopedia of Sexual Behavior:*

Without [emphasis in original] specific sexual experiences, man outside of cultures—that is, so-called feral or natural man—or the extreme social isolate, does not generally engage in sexual behavior upon reaching puberty. There is no sexual instinct in man.[44]

H. C. Resnik and Marvin Wolfgang in *Sexual Behaviors: Social, Clinical, and Legal Aspects:* "One is normally born with a given sex and the capacity to manifest the sex drive, but the expression of that drive is more intimately related to one's culture and social system than any other drive."[45]

---

[43] Wainwright Churchill, *Homosexual Behavior among Males* (New York: 1967), 101.
[44] Robert Frumkin, *The Encyclopedia of Sexual Behavior* (New York: 1967), 439.
[45] H. C. Resnik and Marvin Wolfgang, *Sexual Behaviors: Social, Clinical, and Legal Aspects* (Boston: 1972), 397.

Charles Socarides in "Homosexuality: Basic Concepts and Psychodynamics":

> Homosexuality, the choice of a partner of the same sex for orgastic satisfaction, is not innate. There is no connection between sexual instinct and choice of sexual object. Such an object choice is learned, acquired behavior; there is no inevitable genetically inborn propensity toward the choice of a partner of either the same or opposite sex."[46]

John Money in "Sexual Dimorphism and Homosexual Gender Identity": "Whatever may be the possible unlearned assistance from constitutional sources, the child's psychosexual identity is not written, unlearned, in the genetic code, the hormonal system or the nervous system at birth."[47]

A. Limentani in *Sexual Deviation:* "The development of homosexual attitudes and impulses can be and often [is] used as a defense against neurotic and psychotic processes."[48]

Joyce McDougall in *Sexual Deviation:* "Female homosexuality is an attempt to resolve conflict concerning the two poles of psychic identity; one's identity as a separate individual and one's sexual identity."[49]

William H. Masters, Virginia E. Brown, and Robert C. Kolodny (i.e., Masters and Johnson) in *Human Sexuality:* "The genetic theory of homosexuality has been generally discarded today."[50] "Despite the interest in possible hormone mechanisms in the origin of homosexuality, no serious scientist today suggests that a simple cause-effect relationship applies."[51]

---

[46] Charles Socarides, "Homosexuality: Basic Concepts and Psychodynamcis", *International Journal of Psychiatry* 10 (1972): 118–25.

[47] John Money, "Sexual Dimorphism and Homosexual Gender Identity", *Perspectives in Human Sexuality* (1974): 67.

[48] A. Limentani, in Rosen, *Sexual Deviation*, 197.

[49] Joyce McDougall, in Rosen, *Sexual Deviation*, 206.

[50] William H. Masters, Virginia E. Brown, and Robert C. Kolodny, *Human Sexuality* (Boston: 1984), 319.

[51] Ibid., 320.

George A. Rekers in "The Formation of Homosexual Orientation", an address before the North American Social Science Network Conference:

> At the present time, we may tentatively conclude that the main source for gender and sexual behavior deviance is found in social learning and psychological development variables . . . although we should recognize that there remains the theoretical possibility that biological abnormalities could contribute a potential vulnerability factor in some indirect way.[52]

This summary of opinion voiced over a period of some forty years should dispel the illusion that there is scientific "proof" that homosexuality is inherited.[53] Yet all too often the press persists in suggesting that such proof does exist and that the debate is now over.

I am not the only one concerned with this misrepresentation. Homosexual activist Dennis Altman, in his highly sympathetic book *The Homosexualization of America*, has written:

> Despite press reports suggesting firm evidence of a biological basis for homosexuality, the latest Kinsey Institute study, *Sexual Preference*, claims no more than "at the moment a large body of convincing research appears to suggest a biological foundation for homosexuality, at least among some people." They are impressed with the considerable efforts of biologists, endocrinologists, and physiologists to prove this foundation; I am more

[52] George A. Rekers, "The Formation of Homosexual Orientation", address before the North American Social Science Network Conference, 1987.

[53] Other researchers, while agreeing that homosexuality is not inherited, dispute the neutrality of sexual identity. For example, according to Irving Bieber, "In our view, the human has a capacity for homosexuality, but a tendency towards heterosexuality. The capacity for responsivity to heterosexual excitation is inborn. Courtship behavior and copulatory technique is learned. Homosexuality, on the other hand, is acquired and discovered as a circumventive adaptation for coping with fear of heterosexuality . . . sexual gratification is not renounced; instead, fears and inhibitions associated with heterosexuality are circumvented and sexual responsivity with pleasure and excitement to a member of the same sex develops as a pathologic alternative" (Irving Bieber et al., *Homosexuality, a Psychoanalytic Study of Male Homosexuals* [New York: 1962]).

impressed by the inability of many years of research to amount
to more than "suggestions".[54]

If so many psychotherapists reject the idea that homosexuality is an inherited tendency, how do they think the condition
arises? While the theories are numerous and often contradictory, most share a common assumption that homosexual conduct stems from environmental influences, particularly
familial relationships in early childhood. While Kinsey tended
to view homosexuality as no more than a relatively harmless
sexual preference, many psychotherapists believe that the condition is a "personality disorder", a "perversion", a "defense
mechanism", or a "psychopathology".[55]

The degree to which this abnormal behavior is viewed with
concern depends on several factors, some of them theoretical,
some of them practical. However, while most therapists are
willing to grant that some homosexuals can function well in
society, many also tend to believe that the condition is essentially unhealthy. Some argue that treatment can result in cure;
others are much more pessimistic.[56]

When you read the literature written by these people, you
are aware of just how restrictive the popular dialogue has

[54] Dennis Altman, *The Homosexualization of America* (New York: 1982),
44.

[55] "Although I once believed that exclusive homosexuals are seriously neurotic, considerable experience with treating many of them (and in being
friendly with a number whom I have not seen for psychotherapy) has convinced me that I was wrong! Most fixed homosexuals, I now am convinced,
are borderline psychotic or outright psychotic. In every case I have seen, irrational fear played the leading role in inducing the individual to become homosexual in the first place or inducing him to maintain his early acquired
homophilic conditioning in the second place." (Dr. Albert Ellis, *Homosexuality: Its Causes and Cure*, [New York: 1965]).

[56] "The only effective way of fighting and counteracting homosexuality
would be the wide dissemination of the knowledge that there is nothing glam-
orous about suffering from the disease known as homosexuality, that the disease can be cured, and that this apparently sexual disorder is invariably
coupled with severe unconscious self-damage that will inevitably show up
outside the sexual sphere as well, because it embraces the entire personality"
(Edmund Burglar, *Homosexuality: Disease or Way of Life* [New York: 1962],
281–82).

become, how essentially distorted. These scientists, many of them recognized as authorities in their fields, write as if the pathological nature of homosexuality were an accepted fact, one they could expect to refer to without contradiction. It is important, therefore, that we learn what these people are saying, since they are the ones who deal with homosexual patients on a day-to-day basis.

1. *Homosexuality as Illness*

Perhaps the most authoritative earlier survey of this body of opinion can be found in *Sexual Deviation*,[57] edited by British psychiatrist Ismond Rosen, with contributions from a number of world authorities. Though this book is not written with a popular audience in mind, it is accessible to those of us who are willing to read carefully and to look up words. I have found it very useful in grasping the wide variety of opinion concerning homosexuality and assessing the degree to which each theory is held. Neither Rosen nor his numerous contributors believe that homosexuality is the result of heredity. They also reject the idea that the condition is in any sense normal. But in his introduction Rosen surveys the work of those who argue for hormonal or genetic explanations, granting that what they say may have value in some cases and to some limited degree. His book is a fair and comprehensive overview of the scholarship through the 1970s.

In the introductory essay, "A General Psychiatric Approach to Sexual Deviation", Anthony Wakeling, senior lecturer in psychiatry at Royal Free Hospital Medical College of London, summarizes current psychoanalytical theory. He begins by saying: "It is the persistent and compulsive substitution of some other act for heterosexual and genital intercourse which chiefly characterizes the behavior called sexual deviation."[58] In

---

[57] Rosen, *Sexual Deviation*.
[58] Anthony Wakeling, in Rosen, *Sexual Deviation*, 3.

other words, the conduct he and his colleagues will be describing is not only a "substitute" for normal intercourse but a "persistent and compulsive" one.

Wakeling then lists the main types of sexual deviation:
"These categories include homosexuality, sexual activity with
immature partners of either sex (paedophilia), dead people
(necrophilia), animals (bestiality), or inanimate objects
(fetishism)."[59] Of these deviations, Dr. Wakeling says:

> Clinically, deviant sexual behavior is often associated with an
> impairment of the ability to achieve mutually satisfying rela-
> tionships with adults of the opposite sex, and with the retention
> of childlike patterns of relating to others. In contrast to normal
> sexual behaviour, deviant behaviour is often associated with
> strong affects of guilt and hate. Whereas normal sexual behav-
> iour is more likely to occur in a setting of affection and mutual
> sharing, of equal giving and receiving of pleasure, deviant sex-
> ual behaviour frequently occurs without discrimination as to
> partner, and without consideration to the feelings of others. It
> appears to be dictated more by neurotic or non-sexual than by
> erotic needs, which leads to a large element of compulsiveness
> and risk-taking associated with the behaviour.[60]

If you examine this paragraph carefully, you will begin to
understand the way a significant segment of the psychiatric
community feels about homosexuality and why their account
of this phenomenon is so profoundly different from the view
expressed by homosexuals themselves.

Note that Dr. Wakeling sees sexual deviation as associated
with *failure*, with an inability to achieve heterosexual satisfaction. So homosexuality for him—and indeed for the other
contributors to this volume—is something less than heterosexuality, a poor substitute for the kind of adult relationships
normal to society. In fact, Dr. Wakeling maintains that sexual
deviants are immature and childish in dealing with other people; and that while normal people usually tend to be loving and
caring, deviants, like self-centered children, frequently don't

[59] Ibid.
[60] Ibid., 3–4.

care with whom they have sex, nor are they concerned with the feelings of their partners.

This description does not fit every homosexual, nor does Wakeling say that it does. However, it certainly characterizes the conduct of the large numbers who have frequented the "gay bathhouses", having sex with strangers whose names they don't know and to whom they never speak, sometimes never seeing the person on the other side of the partition, with its impersonal aperture. There is really no comparable phenomenon among heterosexuals (not even in recent years, when singles bars have produced a high degree of casual promiscuity).

In addition, Wakeling makes another important observation: deviant behavior by homosexuals is basically *nonsexual* in nature—that is, it is conduct that expresses some feeling or need other than the erotic. While homosexuals think they are prodigiously sexual, Wakeling maintains that their actions are motivated by hidden impulses they themselves do not understand, and that's why they find no lasting satisfaction in what they do.

Given this description, what is to be said about the American Psychiatric Association's removal of homosexuality from the list of mental illnesses? Here's what Wakeling has to say on the subject of mental health among homosexuals: "As sexuality is intimately interwoven throughout all aspects of personality, it is to be anticipated that deviant sexual behavior will frequently co-exist with profound personality maladjustment, severe neurotic difficulties, and fears of heterosexuality."[61]

This picture, a disturbing one, does not describe every homosexual. Wakefield says that sexual deviation is "also compatible with adaptive social functions and with *elements* of relatively normal heterosexual functioning" (emphasis added), but the examples he offers do not include homosexuality, and he goes on to speak of

[61] Ibid., 4.

an immense gulf between individuals at one end of a spectrum who have never passed beyond an infantile level of psychosexual development, and those well-adjusted individuals at the other end who revert to deviant sexual behaviour only under the impact of severe physical or psychological stress.[62]

Note that those who are "well-adjusted" do not indulge in deviant behavior except when under extreme stress. Thus practicing homosexuals are not at the normal end of Dr. Wakeling's spectrum. They are at the other extreme, classified among those "who have never passed beyond an infantile level of psychosexual development".

Essentially Wakeling is echoing Freud here, and indeed many psychotherapists believe that homosexuality is a form of arrested development. In most theories the growth of the personality toward maturity is to a significant degree retarded by conditions, usually within the family confines, that arise to inhibit the child's maturation. Many theorists regard the first three years of life as the period during which those personality defects are forged that may later lead to alcoholism, drug use, and other forms of addictive behavior, including homosexual acts.

Having confined my attention thus far to scientific theories—both those that promote the idea of biological determinism and those that promote environmental determinism—I must say a word about the limits of approaching the problem of sexuality—or indeed any other human behavior—from a purely scientific standpoint.

It should be clear that many of these theories presuppose the idea that homosexuality is the inevitable result of causes that can be known and to some degree measured. Because of the political controversy surrounding this particular kind of conduct (and the claim that civil or human rights are involved), many people have been willing to accept such a view without questioning the assumption about human nature that underlies

[62] Ibid.

it. All of these theories are "deterministic", and many suggest that human beings have no control over their behavior.

Furthermore, just as there are researchers who find endocrinal explanations for sexual attraction to people of the same sex, so are there researchers who say that suicide can be explained in the same way—or alcoholism, or murder, or being just plain ill-tempered.

"A low level of serotonin seems to be a biochemical marker for those depressed people who are most prone to suicide", says Dr. Herman van Praag, a psychiatrist at the Albert Einstein College of Medicine.[63] Maybe, says Edwin Shneidman of UCLA, but

> [s]ociologists have shown that suicide rates vary with factors like war and unemployment; psychoanalysts argue that it is rage against a loved one that is directed inward; psychiatrists see it as a chemical imbalance. No one approach holds the answer: it is all that and more, including an existential dilemma."[64]

The same argument is given in a different area of human behavior, with the same competing theories, but with one difference: thus far the suicide-as-a-right advocates have not become a formidable political movement (though they do exist).

As for alcoholism, Dr. Frank Siexas, former director of the National Council on Alcoholism, has speculated that "chemical events are going on in a number of different ways which will produce alcoholism".[65] Dr. Ting Kai Li of the Department of Medicine and Biochemistry at Indiana University believes that genetics is responsible for the varying rates in alcoholic metabolism.[66] And there are even twin studies that seem to indicate that the risk for alcoholism in the identical twin of an alcoholic is twice as high as the risk for a fraternal

[63] Quoted in *New York Times* (Oct. 8, 1985).
[64] Ibid.
[65] Quoted in *Boston Globe* (Aug. 8, 1983).
[66] Ibid.

twin of an alcoholic.[67] Others, however, believe that alcoholism is the product of environmental influences, particularly in early childhood.

Again, in the study of alcoholism, the same arguments and divisions exist, the same conflicting authorities speaking confidently from the perspectives of different disciplines. Yet no one is ready to argue that alcoholism is "normal", an "alternate life-style", or a "civil or natural right". There is no "alcoholics' movement", though there are those who would like to see alcoholic drunk drivers exempted from the consequences of their acts because they are not responsible for their actions.

Obesity, anorexia, bad temper, even murder—all these things have been blamed on genetics, hormones, or the irresistible effects of a disruptive early childhood. Such arguments have been going on since Mendel. They will continue until the archangel Gabriel ends the debate with an unexpected blast on his horn.

And as long as the arguments are carried on with some degree of civility and objectivity, we can still learn from one another in making decisions about such matters. As a congressman I have often profited from the arguments and evidence of those with whom I disagree; and sometimes I have even changed my mind. But in dealing with AIDS and the attendant problem of homosexual promiscuity, I have encountered a degree of ferocious irrationality that no other issue has provoked.

I have seen the organized homosexual movement turn every scientific disagreement into a political issue and impugn the integrity and motives of everyone who disagrees with them. I have discovered that radical suppression of scientific opinion can and does exist in this country and that confrontation and belligerence can even change medical diagnosis.

[67] Ibid.

CHAPTER TWO

Homosexuality and the Law

Most of the laws that govern our behavior are not derived from the Constitution but from English common law, which has its origins in the dim past, almost before formal history was written. At one time a good many of the crimes we think of as "civil" were ecclesiastical crimes, that is, crimes against the laws of God as defined in Holy Scripture, and therefore tried in special Church courts.

During the sixteenth century, when Henry VIII broke with Rome, he made the worst of these crimes secular offenses. One of these was murder. Another was sodomy.[1]

When the first great book on the English legal system was written—Blackstone's *Commentaries on the Laws of England*— its author referred to sodomy as "the infamous crime against nature, committed either with man or beast . . . the very mention of which is a disgrace to human nature".[2] This book, published a year before the American Revolution, defines the state of the law at the time of our founding. As in all the nations of Western Europe, sodomy was illegal in the colonies and in the thirteen states of the new nation—and it remained so until 1961, when the first states began to decriminalize homosexual acts.

As of 1984, at least twenty-two of those states have dropped these statutes from their books,[3] and in the remaining states homosexual activists are working night and day to repeal them. These activist forces are also attempting to achieve the

[1] 25 Henry VIII, c. 6 (1553), in Charles Rice, *Legalizing Homosexual Conduct: The Role of the Supreme Court in the Gay Rights Movement* (Washington, D.C.: 1984), 1.

[2] IV W. Blackstone, *Commentaries on the Laws of England* 215–16 (7th ed., 1775), in Rice, 1.

[3] Rice, 1.

same ends through the courts, but thus far the Supreme Court has upheld the right of states to make laws governing such conduct, though the future of these statutes is very much in doubt.

Before examining the current law, however, I would like to discuss the nature of the changes that have taken place over the past twenty-five to thirty years. I would like to try to indicate why, after 450 years of secular prohibition (and another 1,500 of Church condemnation), the United States should begin in the second half of the twentieth century to decriminalize acts that have always been considered a crime against nature as well as against society.

In general, the impulses to rewrite all of criminal law comes originally from the social scientists and more particularly from deterministic theories of human behavior. Such theories are not new to the twentieth century, nor do they constitute the latest breakthrough in progressive thought. In fact, they are of nineteenth-century origin. Dostoevski, in *Crime and Punishment*, discusses such ideas and dismisses them as depriving human beings of the dignity of free will. In the early twentieth century, Theodore Dreiser was beginning to give them literary credence; and by midcentury, deterministic theories of crimality were celebrating their hundredth birthday. But they were just beginning to make an impact on the American legal establishment, and by the end of the 1960s we were in the middle of the era of the Criminal as Victim, when even murderers had come to be regarded as martyrs and hence folk heroes. Lindbergh kidnaper-killer Bruno Hauptmann was lying in his grave 13 months after his conviction, already having been denied his appeal and executed. In contrast, a contemporary serial killer like Ted Bundy was allowed to live on for years, while his victims' bones lay scattered in fields and woods all over the country.

But homosexuality has not been legitimized because of Marxist victimology so much as because of theories developed by other social scientists, by ideological researchers who have investigated the sexual behavior of twentieth-century Americans and, on the basis of their findings, called for sweeping changes in the law. In particular, the sex laws of the United States have in part been changed because of the philosophical climate created by Alfred Kinsey and his followers.

Kinsey published his first famous book, *Sexual Behavior in the Human Male*, in 1948.[4] It purported to be a scientifically devised survey of practices among American men, a kind of sexual equivalent of the Gallup poll. At the time it appeared, many researchers and scholars recognized its severe bias.[5] Kinsey bristled under the criticism, accusing his scientific detractors of being envious or prudish. But curiously, the popular press held Kinsey in awe, proclaiming what many of his peers refused to acknowledge—that what Kinsey had produced was "a landmark study of profound significance".

Years later Kinsey's coauthors Gebhard and Pomeroy would admit that the *Male* volume was weighted in favor of extravagant and bizarre sexual behavior. Here are three ways in which the study was slanted.

- Kinsey used a very large number of prisoners in collecting his 5,300 case histories. His younger assistants tried to tell Kinsey that prisoners behaved differently from people on the outside, that lawbreakers were probably more likely to have led unconventional lives, but Kinsey refused to listen. Later, after the *Male* volume had already been published, he had to admit that they were right.[6]

- Kinsey's interviewees were all volunteers, people who agreed to tell him (or one of his colleagues) their entire sexual history. The famous psychologist Abraham Maslow

[4] Alfred Kinsey et al., *Sexual Behavior in the Human Male* (Philadelphia: 1948).

[5] Wardell Pomeroy, *Dr. Kinsey and the Institute for Sex* (New York: 1972), 283–306.

[6] Paul Gebhard and Alan B. Johnson, *The Kinsey Data: Marginal Tabulations of the 1938–1963 Interviews Conducted by the Institute for Sex Research* (Philadelphia: 1979), 28–29.

told Kinsey that his volunteers were by definition not a representative group, since only certain personality types would readily agree to such private revelations, but again Kinsey refused to listen.[7]

• Contrary to all rules of objective sampling (including his own), Kinsey sought out people he knew to be homosexuals, frequenting their bars, prowling their rooming houses, and even attending their club orgies, because he was so fascinated with their behavior. He gathered literally hundreds of such histories, thereby weighing his study heavily in favor of homosexuals.[8]

This distorted view of American sex habits had a profound effect on the nation's perception of itself at a crucial moment in American history. With World War II just ending (Kinsey's interviewing coincided with the war, an abnormal period in history), we were just beginning to rediscover who we were as a people. Kinsey told us something about ourselves we hadn't known before: we were hypocritical about our sexual behavior, or so it appeared, because Kinsey's studies revealed that an astonishing 10 percent of American males were homosexuals and that 37 percent had had homosexual relations to the point of orgasm.[9] The fact that many of his fellow scientists had faulted Kinsey's methodology and dismissed his findings did not prevent later "sexologists" and public health officials from citing his study as authoritative.

Essentially they argued as follows: everyone is committing adultery, and most men are having homosexual adventures, so how can we possibly outlaw this conduct? You can't have a law that no one obeys. It makes a mockery of law itself. Therefore, anyone prosecuted for sex acts is doing no more than

[7] Abraham Maslow and James M. Sakoda, "Volunteer-Error in the Kinsey Study", *Journal of Abnormal Psychology* (April 1952): 259–62.

[8] Pomeroy, 97–137.

[9] Kinsey, op. cit.

what everyone else is doing. The only difference is, the others aren't getting caught.

Eventually lobbyists for the liberalized sex laws began using this argument in quiet conversations with state legislators around the country, pointing to the widespread acceptance of Kinsey as evidence in courts at every level. The result: most states have modified their criminal codes to eliminate such acts as fornication, adultery, and sodomy, while leaving rape and child molestation on the books.

But there were two things wrong with this argument. First, there is every reason to believe that Kinsey's figures bore little resemblance to reality in 1948. Subsequently, even his followers would admit that the study was flawed.[10]

Second, it simply doesn't follow that just because many people are violating a law, it should therefore be stricken from the books. In fact, we all know of laws that we ourselves violate, yet we still approve of them. The most obvious and oft-cited example is the speed limit on our highways. Regardless of what that limit is, we all exceed it from time to time. We are late for an appointment. We forget to watch the speedometer. We don't see the "Reduce Speed" sign. Almost no one who drives a car is guiltless, though some are deliberately and dangerously irresponsible.

So why don't we abolish the laws? After all, isn't it hypocritical to keep a statute on the books when everyone is violating it? The answer is no, not if the law defines sound behavior for good citizens, not if it contributes significantly to the well-being of society.

Clearly more people violate traffic laws than violate anti-sodomy laws, even granting the truth of Kinsey's highly unreliable figures, yet no one is agitating to remove all traffic laws from the books. So the principle the sex law reformers were citing is a false one and should never have been accepted by intelligent people.

[10] For example, see Gebhard and Johnson.

But there was no powerful pressure group pushing for the abolition of the speed limit or income tax laws during this period, whereas the homosexual network was operating effectively and on a nationwide basis by the early seventies. So sodomy laws were quietly dropped from the books in state after state, sometimes with the rewriting of "outmoded constitutions", sometimes by tacking an amendment onto another bill, a rider never noted by the all-too-compliant press.

Meanwhile, things were happening in the Supreme Court that further altered the general perception of sexuality. In 1965, the Supreme Court made an important ruling in the case of *Griswold* v. *Connecticut*, a challenge to an old law that made it illegal for married couples to use contraceptive devices.

This law—which was clearly unenforceable—was declared unconstitutional because, as Justice William O. Douglas wrote, the privacy of the marriage relationship was being invaded by a law "forbidding the *use* of contraceptives rather than regulating their manufacture or sale. . . . Would we allow the police to search the sacred precincts of marital bedrooms for telltale signs of the use of contraceptives? The very idea is repulsive to the notions of privacy surrounding the marriage relationship"[11] (emphasis in original).

Douglas made his argument in part on the basis of a "right of privacy"; and it was in further defense of that "right", nowhere mentioned in the Constitution or its various amendments, that a series of additional rulings were made. But Justice Douglas declared that "specific guarantees in the Bill of Rights have penumbras, formed by emanations from those guarantees that help give them life and substance".[12]

The more you read this statement, the less sense it makes. Penumbras are the secondary shadows you see under certain circumstances surrounding the darker shadow. But how these "emanate" is anybody's guess. The image is vague and imprecise, as is the thought it is attempting to embody. Yet on this

---

[11] *Griswold* v. *Connecticut*, 381 U.S. 449 (1958), 485–86.
[12] Ibid., 484.

very passage a number of additional decisions were built, including *Roe* v. *Wade*, which declared abortion laws unconstitutional that had been on the books since the beginnings of European settlement in the New World.

Then, in 1972, the Supreme Court ruled that the "right of privacy" in sexual matters extended to unmarried heterosexual couples. The case was *Eisenstadt* v. *Baird*, and the High Court ruled that one William Baird was deprived of equal protection under the law when he was convicted of distributing contraceptives to unmarried couples, a practice forbidden by law, though it was legal to distribute such devices to married couples.

But in addition to citing the often-used equal protection clause of the Fourteenth Amendment, the court also referred to the "right of privacy" recently defined in *Griswold* v. *Connecticut*:

> It is true that in Griswold the right of privacy in question inhered in the marital relationship. Yet the marital couple is not an independent entity with a mind and heart of its own, but an association of two individuals each with a separate intellectual and emotional makeup. If the right of privacy means anything, it is the right of the *individual*, married or single, to be free from unwarranted governmental intrusion into matters so fundamentally affecting a person as the decision whether to bear or beget a child.[13]

It was in this decision, perhaps, that the High Court moved beyond traditional boundaries in a way not immediately apparent to many of those who read the decision. Though the step from *Griswold* to *Eisenstadt* seems logical enough when you consider the idea of privacy as a "right", the decision begs another question with a bit of awkward sophistry when it simply dismisses the age-old prerogative of the community to insist that only married people may licitly have sexual intercourse.

---

[13] *Eisenstadt* v. *Baird*, 405 U.S. 430 (1972), 453.

Since the days of the early Romans and Jews, sexual norms were so defined; and while there may have been times when the rules were widely and easily broken, there was never a time before when legal authorities stepped forward and said, "We no longer have a right to make such rules."

Part of the problem lay in the fact that the Court no longer saw marriage as Christians and Jews had always seen it. Note the Court's denial that the marital couple is "an independent entity". In an important way that is precisely what Western society has always said marriage was. A man and woman "become one flesh". In several important ways the law *does* regard them as "an independent entity". That is why a wife cannot be forced to testify against her husband: because we have prohibitions against self-incrimination, and for purposes of the law the wife is considered identical with the husband. The Court's argument could easily be used to deny couples the prerogative of refusing to take the witness stand against one another.

Once married couples become in the eyes of the law no more than two individuals, each with sexual rights independent of their relationship to one another, then marriage no longer has the same traditional legal status — at least none that can't be claimed by single people who are living together. Thus *Eisenstadt* v. *Baird* was the real ground breaker for the sexual revolution, the decision that separated sex from marriage and opened the door for *Roe* v. *Wade*, the decision that said because of the right of privacy established in *Griswold* and *Eisenstadt*, women could elect to kill their unborn children, regardless of longtime state statutes.

But what about homosexual intercourse? Have the courts extended the right of privacy to include sexual acts between persons of the same sex?

So far they have not. As a matter of fact, they have thus far upheld the right of states to pass sodomy laws in Virginia, Texas, and Georgia. But that does not mean that at some future time, when the climate is right, they might not choose to make a final disposition of this question in favor of the sodomites. Here is how one authority on the subject sees the current state of the law:

> In sum, the Supreme Court cases to date concerning sex, marriage, and the family do not support the view that there is a right to engage in any form of sexual expression so long as the actors are adults and the conduct is consensual and private. The Court has recognized the importance of freedom to make decisions in regard to marriage, child-rearing, whether to bear or beget a child and whether to continue or terminate a pregnancy. The realm of choice involved in these cases, however, is *not* sexual expression. Individual justices have explicitly affirmed that regulation of promiscuous or "illicit" sexual relationships is a permissible and legitimate state end. Those who have expressed doubts about the legitimacy of state regulation of consensual sexual activity are in a minority.[14]

An optimistic view, but who would have thought twenty-five years ago that the courts would have denied the states the right to pass laws forbidding abortion? In reviewing the history of this odd and arbitrary decision, I notice that the groundwork was laid for it in the activism of the "women's liberation movement", with their marches, their slogans, and their lawsuits at the local level. Had they not continually harangued the courts, they would never have caught the attention of the justices, who since the beginning of the Republic have been "political" in their interpretation of the law. Abortion was one of the most important political goals of the feminists, and they never stopped demanding that their petitions be granted. One sees in all this the echo of a parable: that of the widow and the unjust judge; but perhaps it is also the foreshadowing of future events.

Homosexual activists have been following the same tactics over the past few years. While the High Court has not yet granted them what they want—a ruling that the U.S. Constitution guarantees them the right to sodomize—they are filing

---

[14] Katz, "Sexual Morality and the Constitution: People v. Onofre", 46, *Albany Law Review* 311 (1982): 338–39.

suits in courts throughout the country. They are filling the legal publications with their rhetoric and racking up an impressive string of victories in places where local law is favorable to their interests and where judges are likely to be sympathetic or intimidated.

Here are just a few of the legal actions they have initiated over the past several years and some of the outcomes:

National Gay Rights Advocates (NGRA) has completed a successful action against Pacific Northwest Bell on behalf of a homosexual, Mitchell Foshay, who applied for funeral leave when his male lover's father died. Pacific Northwest Bell told him that only married employees were eligible for such leave when a household member's family dies. NGRA filed a complaint with the Seattle Human Rights Department, which ruled that Foshay had the same rights as a married person to receive funeral leave. [15]

In the same vein, a lesbian in New York took three days from her work at the Legal Aid Society when her lover's mother died. According to *Lambda Update* she took this time off "to assist with funeral arrangements and to offer emotional support to her lover and other family members". When she returned to work, she requested the three-day "bereavement leave" guaranteed for "the death of a mother-in-law". Her request was denied, whereupon she filed a complaint against the Legal Aid Society with the New York Commission on Human Rights, charging "discrimination based on sexual orientation". [16]

The National Gay Rights Advocates now routinely refer to homosexuals living together as "family partners", a phrase

---

[15] *National Gay Rights Advocates (NGRA) Newsletter* (Autumn 1987).
[16] *Lambda Update* (Fall 1987), 10.

they have adopted for reasons that should be apparent from the following cases:

- Boyce Hinman and Larry Beaty have been cohabiting for fourteen years in Sacramento, California. They own a home together, have a joint bank account, and have made each other beneficiaries in wills and life insurance policies. Recently, when they applied for additional homeowners' policies, they were told by Farmers Insurance Company that they would be charged $260, though had they been married the charge would have been $130. Naturally they are suing, and NGRA is handling the suit of these "family partners".[17]

- Meanwhile, in Wisconsin Jerri Linn Phillips, a lesbian, is trying to obtain group insurance for her "family partner", Lori J. Tommerup. They have lived together since 1983 and pool all their resources, so NGRA is representing the couple in their appeal of the refusal to grant group rates by the Wisconsin Department of Health and Human Services.[18]

In a First Amendment case of great significance, the Lambda Defense League, a homosexual advocacy group, has sued the Gannett Satellite Information Network because one of its newspapers, the *Green Bay Press-Gazette*, refused to accept an advertisement for "Among Friends", an organization serving "rural lesbians and gay men".

Of this action, *Lambda Update* says:

> The case also presents a challenge to the First Amendment defense asserted by the newspaper: that freedom of the press allows them to discriminate. The complaint has been amended to include two new plaintiffs, Peggy and Tracy Vandeveer, a lesbian couple who had also submitted an ad to *The Green Bay Press-Gazette* to sell gay and lesbian motto T-shirts.[19]

[17] *NGRA Newsletter* (1987).
[18] Ibid.
[19] *Lambda Update* (Fall 1987), 11.

Lambda Legal Defense Fund refused to give up in the case of
Madsen v. *Robert Erwin et al.*, even though the Supreme Judicial Court has ruled that the *Christian Science Monitor* was "an
arm of the church" and therefore had a religious right to fire
Madsen because she was a lesbian. The Supreme Judicial
Court did allow the defendant to amend and pursue her tort
claims, and *Lambda Update* reported that the complaint was
filed "seeking money damages for invasion of privacy, defa-
mation, intentional infliction of emotional distress, intentional
interference with contractual relations, and intentional interference with advantageous relations".[20]

Students at Arizona State University did not want to grant
funding to the Lesbian and Gay Academic Union, a homosexual student group. Lambda Legal Defense Fund intervened
and forced the university to conduct "annual legal education
for members of the student body which will include a discussion of the impermissibility of discrimination based on sexual
orientation". The university has also agreed to co-sponsor
with the Lesbian and Gay Academic Union a series of lesbian
and gay forums—i.e., educational programs on issues such as
violence and discrimination, lesbian and gay history, and life-
style issues.[21]

In *Hernandez* v. *Immigration and Naturalization Service*, the
Lambda Defense League is attempting to help five Cubans
from the Mariel boatlift obtain legal status. The five have been
denied permanent residence because their passports indicate
they are homosexuals. The Immigration Act excluded homosexuals of both sexes, but Lambda set out to change all that.
In their *Update* they say: " 'Hernandez' is representative of
perhaps thousands of other Cubans who came to the United
States as part of the Cuban Flotilla Crisis of 1980 and who
have now been in the country long enough to apply for a

[20] Ibid.
[21] Ibid., 5.

status change but whose applications are being denied because of the gay issue." They further report: "We are continuing to work closely with Congressman Barney Frank (D-MA) in making use of changes he secured in the new immigration laws that can be of help to Hernandez and other similarly situated persons, and possibly other gay people with immigration problems."[22]

National Gay Rights Advocates have announced they will file a lawsuit against an Orlando, Florida, physician "for breach of medical confidentiality". It seems that Dr. Herminio Orizondo informed the employer of Jim Kautz that Kautz had tested positive for the AIDS virus. Kautz, a surgical technician, was subsequently fired from his job.[23]

Lambda has filed a suit in California Superior Court on behalf of two homosexual couples who were prohibited from "touch dancing" at Disneyland. A policeman at the famous theme park attempted to stop the homosexuals from dancing together on the floor, telling them that "touch dancing" was only for heterosexuals.[24]

In California Governor George Deukmejian signed into law a bill that upgraded certain crimes from misdemeanors to felonies *if the motive for the crime could be identified as "homophobia"*. In some cases the sentence could be raised to three years in prison if the attack was motivated by "hate because of sexual orientation".[25]

The Lambda Legal Defense Fund has announced a contemplated challenge of sodomy laws in Florida and Michigan. Though the Supreme Court has thus far upheld sodomy laws,

[22] Ibid., 10.
[23] *NGRA Newsletter* (1987).
[24] *Lambda Update* (March, 1988), 8.
[25] Peter Freiberg, *Advocate* (Dec. 22, 1987), 11.

it has been by a narrow margin, and the homosexuals will continue to push on this issue, knowing that one victory will wipe out all the defeats of the past.[26]

Along those same lines, Terry Adams and Paul Edmonds filed suit against Standard Oil of Ohio (Sohio) for discrimination in employment practices. When Adams, a supervisor, recommended promotions for a number of homosexuals, she was threatened with a cut in pay by her manager, who called the homosexuals "nothing but a bunch of cry-babies". Edmonds, one of those refused promotion, said he "became despondent" in the wake of the action and quit. Both are suing Sohio under Section 1101 of the California Labor Code, which makes it illegal to discriminate in employment matters on the basis of "political activity".

So how does this apply to Adams and Edmonds?

They are arguing that since the California Supreme Court has ruled that coming out of the closet is a "political activity", all discrimination by private employers on the basis of homosexuality could be declared illegal.

Their lawyer, Allen French, puts it this way: "If we win, lawsuits like this can be brought all over California and not just in areas where local ordinances ban job discrimination."[27]

The National Gay Rights Advocates is developing "a model privacy statute" to replace sodomy laws now on the books in more than twenty states. As NGRA explains in its newsletter: "The statute is an innovative approach to sodomy reform and is the first such model legislation to be drafted since the Model Panel Code of 1955. Accompanying the statute will be a report detailing the fiscal impact of sodomy laws on a state's economy."[28]

---

[26] *Lambda Update* (March, 1988), 11.
[27] *Washington Blade* (Jan. 29, 1988), 17.
[28] *NGRA Newsletter* (1987).

I. The "Hate Crime" Bill

The House of Representatives, of which I am a member, passed a bill on May 18, 1988, that would mandate the Justice Department to collect state and local statistics about crimes based on race, religion, ethnicity, or "homosexuality or heterosexuality". Many people in Congress failed to understand the extent to which this bill was devised and initially sponsored by the homosexual community rather than by the other minorities mentioned in the bill.

As a matter of fact, it was the National Gay and Lesbian Task Force that first presented the idea to the National Institute of Justice (NIJ) in 1985. The NIJ, which is an official part of the Department of Justice, eventually provided the funds used by Abt and Associates of Cambridge, Massachusetts, to run a study to determine the number of "attacks" against homosexuals as well as other ethnic and religious groups. The results: homosexuals reported more such attacks by far than any other category.

Armed with these statistics, the National Gay and Lesbian Task Force (NGLTF) contacted a number of sympathetic congressmen and began to lobby the House and Senate. They also enlisted the support of the American Psychological Association, the American Civil Liberties Union, and the American Jewish Congress.

A number of liberal organizations banded together, coordinated by Kevin Berrill, director of the National Gay and Lesbian Task Force's Anti-violence Project. These organizations included religious, professional, civil rights, and other activist groups.

According to Congressman Barney Frank, who is openly homosexual, the attorney general of Maine, James Tierney (D.), persuaded twenty-nine other state attorneys general to send letters supporting the bill.

It was difficult, of course, to oppose the bill without being called "racist" and "antisemitic". However, several of us, who saw the ultimate purpose in the bill and its potentially damaging effects on the other minorities listed, did what we could to put the legislation in proper perspective.

Congressman George Gekas (R. Pa.) introduced an amendment that would have removed the phrase "sexual orientation" from the bill, thus leaving those groups that were the victims of crimes because of factors over which they had no control. But the House rejected the Gekas amendment in favor of one by Rep. John Miller (R. Wash.) that changed "sexual orientation" to "homosexual or heterosexual", the version that eventually passed.

Congressman Miller's amendment also stipulated that nothing in the bill could be used as the basis for allowing federal antidiscrimination lawsuits alleging sexual-orientation bias. The homosexuals opposed that provision but knew very well that they had achieved a signal victory and had taken the first step toward inclusion of homosexuals in the next revision of the Civil Rights Bill. Kevin Berrill acknowledged that while the bill that eventually passed was not precisely what his coalition wanted (it did, for example, contain the Miller amendment), they were pleased that for the first time legislation was passed that specifically addressed the issue of "antigay bias". Urvashi Vaid of the NGLTF echoed those sentiments in saying that it was the first time the House had passed a bill of specific concern to the homosexual community.

And how right they were.

Of course, most of my colleagues missed the danger in this bill, seeing it as a means of keeping a running record of bigotry in the country, on the surface not a bad thing to do, even if expensive. But twenty-nine of us saw at least two things wrong with such legislation, and consequently we voted against it.

First, we studied the report by Abt and Associates and saw what had happened. The homosexual community, which sponsored the bill in the first place, had been building up a list of complaints all over the country precisely for this kind of record. For example, in support of the bill, the *Washington Post* had printed a story that listed 232 attacks against homosexuals in the District of Columbia alone. But a closer examination of the figures indicated that 144 of these "attacks" were *verbal*. Thus, a casual street epithet from a passerby, perhaps in response to a sexual overture, is immediately reported to the police and becomes a statistic in the war to imbue homosexuals with special rights. It is small wonder that the homosexuals were listed as having led all other "minorities" in suffering from "hate crimes". How many religious and ethnic groups were alerted to the upcoming study? And how many in the future will be urged to report such verbal exchanges? You can be certain that as these statistics are developed, homosexuals will grab all the headlines, while Blacks, Jews, and others will seem less and less unfairly victimized by comparison.

Second, the bill shifts the focus on crime from the most important aspect to something less significant. According to this legislation, "motive" rather than "behavior" becomes the most important factor in classifying crimes. Thus the nature of the crime itself is deemphasized. Let me illustrate.

You are sitting in a restaurant and a man sitting at the next table mistakenly believes you are someone who has been talking about him behind his back. Despite the fact that you've never seen him before and tell him so, he grabs a vase and breaks it over your head, fracturing your skull and putting you in the hospital.

Down the street, a man sits in another restaurant and over-hears a homosexual conversation that spoils his appetite. Because he simply doesn't approve of homosexual conduct and is angered that he has had to listen to a particularly loud and graphic description of such behavior, he picks up a vase and clobbers the homosexual, fracturing his skull and putting him in the hospital.

Under the new bill, the one crime would be recorded and published in a special report from the Department of Justice, thereby assigning it a higher priority in the public consciousness than the other crime. And, if this kind of reporting has the effect the homosexuals hope it will, then a law will subsequently be passed that makes the second crime a federal offense and attaches to it additional risks and penalties.

But let us take another hypothetical case in order to point out an additional problem in this business of recording and publishing statistics on crimes against homosexuals. You are walking down the street, minding your own business, when a person of the same sex accosts you and propositions you. Unnerved and angered, you offer a reply that indicates you find deviate sexual behavior disgusting.

Angered by your remarks (which are clearly "homophobic"), the homosexual goes to the nearest police station and turns you in. Whether or not you are apprehended and prosecuted is irrelevant. You have become an anonymous statistic in the Justice Department's report on "hate crimes".

It is important to note that a strong verbal rebuff of a heterosexual solicitation would not, under this bill, be reported at all, except in the unlikely event that the offended expressed disgust with the very heterosexuality of the aggressor.

If this bill ultimately leads to the kind of civil rights legislation passed in a growing number of states and municipalities, then we will see not only a new kind of warfare waged against normal people by the homosexuals but also a diminution of respect for civil rights legislation in general, with a consequent undermining of protection to those minorities who have been discriminated against because of accidents of birth.

In 1989, the same bill was reintroduced, and instead of seeing its essential irrelevance, the House once again approved it, though this time by a slightly smaller majority. During the debate I offered an amendment that would have restricted "hate crimes" to those groups covered by the 1964 Civil Rights Act, but even Republicans voted against the exclusion of homosexuals, believing that somehow an enormous number of criminal acts were involved, that they were actually in great danger.

Yet the NGTLF *Task Force Report* admitted that in 1988 approximately 77 percent of all "hate crimes" committed against homosexuals were verbal and that nationwide during an entire year they could only find 885 cases where "physical assaults" were involved. Even if you trust their figures, this is a miniscule number when compared to the violence perpetrated against children in this country—some of these crimes committed by homosexual pedophiles.

The Office of Management and Budget has estimated that this bill will cost taxpayers between $1 million and $10 million. Assuming that homosexuals are correct in saying that they are the most victimized group—and a recent issue of the *American Psychologist* seems to support this contention—how much does it cost us to log each crime committed against them? An unconscionable amount, I would suggest, a bribe to appease homosexual activists and to further their ultimate goal, which is special protection under the law.

In summary, the establishment of a force to record and report "hate crimes" will lead to the following: innumerable reports of crimes against homosexuals, orchestrated by activist organizations around the country; the corresponding relegation of crimes against other minorities to the back burner; agitation for a "gay civil rights bill" in the next session of Congress, with the "rising tide of crimes against homosexuals" offered as the justification; and a rash of television programs on the subject, with the Justice Department's report as the stated occasion.

II. AIDS Litigation

Of course, AIDS has presented the homosexual legal force with new challenges—and new opportunities. When the disease was first discovered, it was called "Gay Related Immune

Deficiency Syndrome" (GRIDS) because it seemed to be confined to homosexuals. Thus, from the beginning the homosexual community had a proprietory attitude toward the
disease. Then, after it began to spread into the heterosexual
community, the homosexuals recognized the imminent possibility that if traditional public health service measures were
adopted in dealing with what was now being called "AIDS",
their community would be the subject of considerable scrutiny
by health officials.

To clarify just what I mean here, let me describe briefly the
standard procedures used in the past in the treatment of such
sexually transmitted diseases as syphilis and gonorrhea. Per-
fected by Dr. Thomas Parran, Franklin Roosevelt's Surgeon
General, they were rigorously applied throughout the nation,
particularly in the case of syphilis, which by 1930 was epidemic in this country.[29]

The first thing Parran prescribed was routine testing for
syphilis wherever medical examinations were conducted—
during hospital admissions, in regular checkups at the physician's office, and at physical examinations for job applications
and military service. During the 1930s and early 1940s the federal government alone tested literally tens of millions of people
(more than 30 million in a single year), and some states initiated mandatory test laws. Alabama, for example, passed a law
requiring every citizen between the ages of fifteen and fifty to
be tested, and the federal government helped Alabama admin-
ister the program.

American industry also cooperated in an attempt to stamp
out this widespread and costly disease. Whole industries were
tested, from the president of the corporation down to the latest
recruit. While there were some complaints, by and large the
American people reacted as they had always reacted when
faced by an epidemic: they submitted themselves to public
health authorities, knowing that in time of great crisis every-

[29] Thomas Parran, *Shadow on the Land: Syphilis* (New York: 1936).

one has to make some sacrifices for the health and survival of the community at large.

Those people who argue that AIDS is unique because of the stigma it brings to its victims simply don't understand the recent history of this country. Up until the past thirty years, open sexual promiscuity was unacceptable conduct in respectable society. To be sure, people violated the rules then as now, but they did so as privately as possible, because exposure would have meant significant loss of respect in the community.

As for venereal disease, while it existed in many respectable families, it was universally regarded as the worst kind of disgrace. Syphilis was so stigmatized during the 1930s that the word could not even be pronounced over radio.

Yet Parran introduced and implemented a program of testing for syphilis, and Americans accepted it with only minimal assurances of confidentiality, though Parran did not allow his public health officials to release records, and the security of medical information never became the political issue that it is today.

In fact, the manner in which the war on syphilis was conducted is the best possible argument in favor of widespread testing for HIV. The American medical profession has always acted responsibly in such matters, yet homosexuals are hysterical on the subject, claiming that if routine testing is inaugurated, they will somehow be the victims of widespread betrayal—that their names will be leaked by unscrupulous health officials, and as a consequence they will lose their jobs, be evicted from their homes, and eventually be shipped off to some desert island. Instead of carefully explaining to these poor people that such a thing has never happened and why it never will, our Public Health Service officials have indulged homosexual fears by themselves opposing testing.

The second thing that Parran advocated and promoted as Surgeon General was contact tracing. Clearly syphilis was being spread by intercourse. If testing turned up one case, then tracing that one person's sexual contacts might yield additional cases, thus magnifying the effects of the testing program many times. So Parran pushed public health officials at every level to trace the contacts of those who tested positive, male and female alike.

Of course there were those who suggested that testing be made voluntary, but Parran would have none of that. In his book, *Shadow on the Land: Syphilis*, Parran published a chart to show how poorly voluntary testing fared when measured against mandatory or routine testing. In circumstances where mandatory testing was in force, forty-four cases per thousand were discovered, while in circumstances where testing was voluntary, .6 cases per thousand were discovered.[30]

Routine testing and contact tracing formed the basis for Parran's attack on venereal disease, and by the end of World War II the disease appeared to be on its way toward extinction. Some people argue that this dramatic reduction in infection rate was the result of penicillin. As a matter of fact, the advent of penicillin probably ended all chance that the disease would be stamped out, because with a one-shot treatment available, states began to abolish premarital blood tests, and hospitals and other health care institutions stopped routine testing on admission. The result: the infectious syphilis rate has skyrocketed in recent years and is one of our chief medical problems.

Yet the homosexual community is adamantly opposed to AIDS testing and contact tracing, chiefly because of their fear of persecution. When confronted with the success of earlier syphilis measures, they argue: there was a purpose to testing and contact tracing for syphilis and gonorrhea because they were curable. If you found out someone had the disease, then you could give them a shot and end their misery, but since AIDS is incurable, there is no reason either to test people or to trace their contacts. All you can do, after all, is tell them they're going to die.

[30] Ibid.

The more you think about such an argument, the more you question the humanity of those who make it. The very fact that AIDS is fatal is the most compelling argument for testing. Surely anyone who was infected with the virus would want to know it in order to avoid transmitting it to someone else, no matter how casual the contact. To argue that people would not behave in such a fashion is to underestimate the whole human race.

The same would be true of contact tracing. The more infected people who are aware of their condition, the less likely they will be to spread the disease. Or so I would think, judging from married couples I have known, who would make any sacrifice, give up any pleasure, to protect the life of their mate. If homosexuals want to argue the contrary, then I would like to know on whose observed behavior they base their conclusions.

Yet this is their position—that testing and contact tracing must not be initiated, and that the most important objective of all in the midst of this epidemic is not the prevention of disease but the protection of victims against potential persecution by the community at large.

Thus, while in effect demanding that the nation forget about cancer and heart disease in order to pour greater funds into AIDS research, homosexuals say that testing would be too costly, suggesting that a national program would cost twenty-five to fifty dollars per person, when the armed forces are now testing all inductees for less than five dollars per person.

In addition to these arguments, the homosexuals are also taking a number of legal actions all over the country to make certain that no one tries to inaugurate traditional health policies in dealing with AIDS. Indeed, if published reports of the National Gay Rights Advocates and the Lambda Defense Fund are any indication, a majority of the actions now filed by these groups concern AIDS rather than merely homosexuality.

Here are some of the cases in which these organizations have been involved over the past twenty-four months.

NGRA is now trying to force the federal government to stop prohibiting aliens who are HIV infected from entering this country. Currently no one who tests positive for the AIDS virus can immigrate to this country or become a permanent citizen. According to its newsletter, NGRA argues "that the rule would do virtually nothing to stop the spread of AIDS in the U.S."[31]

The word *virtually* is significant here, since NGRA will not be so foolish as to say that it will have no effect *whatsoever* on the spread of the disease. So how many people does that word *virtually* send to their graves? Wouldn't one life saved be sufficient to institute such a policy? I would think so. Yet the homosexuals disagree. They are more concerned about the possibility—and note it is just a possibility—that foreign governments might retaliate and not allow AIDS-infected Americans to go abroad.

Does this mean that the NGRA is willing to allow X number of Americans to contract AIDS from foreign immigrants and die so that those already in this country who have contracted the disease can still take Mediterranean cruises? That seems to be what they are saying.

But they also say something else that bears examination: "Also, most nations have very poor facilities for testing, and do not perform confirmatory tests. Thus, most people who will be excluded will in fact be false 'positives'."[32]

Again, we see the illogic bordering on madness that is to be found in much homosexual literature. The statement above could be true only if more than 50 percent of all Elisa tests showed up as false positives the first time around. Think about it. Yet in point of fact, false positives are extremely rare in the Elisa test (fewer than 1 in 100,000). So how could it possibly be true that "most people" who show up positive in countries without confirmatory tests are really false positives?

Yet homosexuals continue to make such statements, and no one in the public health service seems willing to step forward

[31] *NGRA Newsletter* (1987).
[32] Ibid.

and defend the actions of the federal government, which are designed to save American lives.

Texas Bankers Life and Loan Insurance decided that hence-forth its major medical insurance policy would contain the fol-lowing exception: "We do not pay for Acquired Immune Deficiency Syndrome." NGRA has objected to this policy and has filed a formal complaint with the Texas State Board of Insurance.[33]

This is not the first time NGRA has intervened to prevent an insurance company from making such a business decision. Previously they had filed a complaint against American Ser-vice Life Insurance Company (ASLIC) with the California Department of Insurance. It seems that ASLIC had announced in promotional materials that the company would not cover expenses for "any disease which was sexually transmitted".[34] In the past insurance companies have been allowed to exclude high-risk behavior and its consequences from normal cover-age.

In 1984 the Lambda Defense League filed a complaint with the Office of Civil Rights of the U.S. Department of Health and Human Services, charging that Charlotte (N.C.) Memorial Hospital discriminated against a registered nurse who was put on involuntary medical leave because she had what *Lambda Update* described as "a pre-AIDS condition".

After investigating the charges for two years, the Office of Civil Rights found that discrimination had indeed occurred. The nurse with the "pre-AIDS condition", however, had died almost six months earlier.[35]

In New Jersey Judge Burrell Ives Humphreys ruled that a land-lord could not refuse to rent an apartment to three homosex-uals whom he suspected of having AIDS. Judge Humphreys

[33] Ibid.
[34] Ibid.
[35] *Lambda Update* (Fall, 1987), 9.

declared that AIDS is a "handicap" and therefore falls under protection of New Jersey's antidiscrimination laws.[36]

In New York two doctors signed a contract to buy a ground-floor co-op in the apartment house where they lived. They intended to use the street-level apartment as an office, and the principal owner agreed to help them reclassify the property for commercial use. Then he found out that at least one of the doctors was treating AIDS patients, and he refused to cooperate in the reclassification.

Lambda Defense League and the New York City Human Rights Commission both filed briefs under the New York Human Rights law, which forbids "AIDS-based discrimination".[37]

In White Plains, New York, a pharmacist was denied employment at a public hospital because he had tested positive for the AIDS virus, a fact hospital officials determined by checking his medical records without his permission. He complained to the New York State Division of Human Rights and to the U.S. Department of Health and Human Services, "alleging discrimination on the basis of a perceived handicap".

Lambda Defense League sees the possibilities in this action: "The Human Rights Division complaint can hopefully be the first to set a statewide precedent on seropositivity as a handicap under the NY Human Rights law."[38]

Lambda lists as a "VICTORY" the ruling by the Florida Supreme Court that the District Court of Appeals was correct in denying "a discovery request" for the names and addresses of blood donors by the estate of a man who "allegedly contracted AIDS" through a transfusion and as a consequence died.

[36] *Advocate* (May 26, 1987), 25.
[37] *Lambda Update* (Fall, 1987), 10.
[38] Ibid., 9.

The appellate court ruled that the dead man's interest in the information was "slight" compared to the privacy interests of the donors and the societal interests in encouraging blood donors.

Lambda submitted an *amicus* brief at the Supreme Court level.[39]

Northwest Airlines, which recently banned in-flight smoking, has agreed to drop a policy that refused tickets to passengers with AIDS. The airline took this action after the National Gay Rights Advocates represented Leonard Matlovich, who had been denied a ticket on those grounds.

At first Northwest revised its policy to require all passengers with AIDS to present a medical certificate indicating they are "noninfectious". They also recorded the AIDS diagnosis in their computers.

NGRA threatened to sue even with the revised regulations, and Northwest was forced to issue a policy statement that "the HIV or AIDS virus is not contagious in casual contact. Northwest will not deny passage to a person with AIDS."[40]

The number of legal actions now being pursued by homosexuals is staggering. They are clearly among the most litigious people in the country, and they will go back into court time and time again when they suffer setbacks on such issues as state sodomy laws. The Lambda Legal Defense Fund and the National Gay Rights Advocates are extremely well financed, and they frequently receive valuable aid from the American Civil Liberties Union. The three organizations constitute a legal phalanx unmatched by any pressure group in the country, and state, local, or private interests aligned against them are often outgunned. More and more lawyers are advising the opponents of homosexual interests to negotiate, compromise, and even surrender rather than to enter into lengthy court

[39] Ibid., 8.
[40] *NGRA Newsletter* (1987).

actions. On their part, the homosexual legal organizations are finding more and more reasons to persist in their actions, so they continue their solicitation for funds, and their constituency continues to be supportive.

This obsessive perseverance would be admirable if it were for a cause that merited it. Certainly it has been effective. Homosexuals have won many local and state battles and are on the verge of winning a stunning and final victory on the national level, a federal "gay rights bill" that will have enormous repercussions in our daily lives. Here are just some of the things that could happen if such a bill were signed into law.

First, we must remember that if homosexuality is treated in precisely the same way that race has been treated, then all of the restrictions and imperatives now a part of our civil rights guarantees to minorities will be immediately and automatically applicable to those who practice deviant behavior with members of the same sex.

Every business, manufacturing plant, shop, and service vendor will be put on notice that homosexuals must be hired regardless of the moral or religious convictions of the employer. If Mom and Pop think that sodomy is a sin and refuse to hire a homosexual to help out in their candy store, then they can be fined and locked up in jail. If a heterosexual and a homosexual apply for the same job, then a personnel director will have to hire the homosexual or run great risks. Since homosexuals are highly litigious, think what the business world will be like after the Gay Civil Rights Act has taken effect.

Rooming houses and private clubs will also be affected, as they are already in Washington, D.C., where it is illegal to exclude someone just because he or she is homosexual. The Supreme Court has already upheld the constitutionality of such laws, so we cannot expect any judicial relief once the legislation is passed.

Furthermore, a lot of business and financial matters will be affected as the result of such legislation, some of these matters relatively unimportant, some of them central to the way our society is now structured. For one thing, homosexuals will undoubtedly be allowed to file joint tax returns and qualify for the same tax breaks that married couples, by virtue of their edifying role in society, now receive.

Then, too, homosexuals would be eligible to receive lower insurance rates and other fringe benefits now reserved for married couples. Some of the lower rates are predicated on actuarial charts that show married people live longer and are sick less often than single people, even those who cohabit. These perquisites are therefore available to married couples because of the stability they bring to the community. Whether or not homosexual couples are as stable (or as stabilizing) will be irrelevant. The policies will probably have to be rewritten to accommodate homosexual domestic arrangements. All of this will cost other taxpayers and insurance policy holders additional money, since the rates and benefits will be predicated on social policy rather than vital statistics.

As a matter of fact, it is quite possible that under new legislation homosexuals will be permitted to marry. At that point, they will then have the legal right to be considered equally and without prejudice when applying to adopt children, something that even a gay rights advocate like Michael Dukakis opposes. Nothing seems riskier to social stability than to turn our youngsters over to these troubled people, who, according to many authorities, have enough difficulty coping with their own problems without taking on the additional responsibility of rearing children. Yet after the passage of a Gay Rights Bill, adoption agencies will have no choice in the matter.

Speaking of children, school curricula will have to be revised where they are not already depicting sodomy as normal and a practice acceptable to society. Teachers will have to be hired with an eye toward "sexual orientation", making certain that enough deviates are on the faculty to provide potentially homosexual youths with "role models".

Extracurricular activities will also have to reflect the new status of homosexuality under the law. There will be homosexual clubs in every school, as there already are in Los Angeles and a few other places, and speakers will be invited to campus to talk to assemblies about the virtues of the homosexual life.

Of course, religious institutions will not be exempt from such required gestures in the direction of homosexuality. Because of the Grove City Bill, even church schools whose students receive government loans will have to hire homosexuals on their faculties and subsidize homosexual activities on campus, something that has already happened at Georgetown University.

These legal changes, which in a few months would stand the Judeo-Christian Tradition of 3,000 years on its head, are what the National Gay and Lesbian Task Force and other organizations have been working for, what these people have specifically stated as their goals. As Jeff Levi put it during their Washington rally in October of 1987:

> The demands of the March on Washington reflect what [the] agenda will be in the years ahead. They include passage of the gay and lesbian rights bill, an executive order dealing with that branch's discriminatory policies—from the military to security clearances; passage of similar measures at the state level as well as repeal of sodomy laws.
> But our agenda is becoming broader than that: we are no longer seeking just a right to privacy and a protection from wrong. We also have a right—as heterosexual Americans already have—to see government and society affirm our lives. Now that is a statement that may make some of our liberal friends queasy. But the truth is, until our relationships are recognized in the law—through domestic partner legislation or the definition of beneficiaries, for example—until we are provided with the same financial incentives in tax law and government programs to affirm our family relationships, then we will not have achieved equality in American society.[41]

If you think all of this is rhetoric or fantasy, remember that over 65 cities in the nation have already adopted such laws, and thus far the High Court has upheld them. In addition,

---

[41] From a speech to the National Press Club (October 10, 1987).

every one of the candidates running for the Democratic nomination in 1988, in replying to a questionnaire by the National Gay and Lesbian Task Force, said he would sign such a bill into law if it passed.

As for the eventual nominee, Michael Dukakis, in an advertisement placed in a New York homosexual newspaper by his campaign organization, he pledged:

> As President, I will fight for federal legislation to add a prohibition against discrimination based on sexual orientation to the existing protections of the 1964 Civil Rights Act.
>
> No American should live in fear of losing a job, of being denied housing, or any opportunity available to others because of his or her sexual orientation. Gay and lesbian citizens deserve the full rights and protections and freedoms guaranteed to all Americans.[42]

Should Michael Dukakis, had he been elected, or any President of the United States, sign a Gay Rights Act into law, then the legislative and the executive branches of government would have effectively overruled the judicial branch, which has clearly stated that in the case of sodomy laws, the Tenth Amendment is still in effect, granting the rights of states to regulate the sexual conduct of citizens in certain broad areas. It is important to note that these two branches have not yet teamed up to restore some kind of prayer in schools, an action that, according to polls, the American people would approve by more than 80 percent.

A Gay Rights Bill, then, would pit the branches of government against one another and force a constitutional crisis of sorts, one that would probably leave the American people bewildered and relatively helpless. Clearly one way to diminish the likelihood of such a confrontation would be to elect chief executives and legislators who would oppose a Gay Rights Bill of any sort. And in that respect, the American people are all powerful.

---

[42] Advertisement in *New York Native* (Apr. 18, 1988).

CHAPTER THREE

The Religious Issue

It has been said that the reason Gandhi was able to force the British to grant India political freedom was because England was still a Christian nation with a conscience. Had they tried the same tactics in dealing with the Soviet Union, the Mahatma and his chief followers would immediately have disappeared, never to be heard of again.

And it is some measure of the Judeo-Christian foundation of the United States that as a nation we are ready to feel a deep sympathy for the plight of homosexuals and to put the best possible construction on their motivation and actions. Have homosexuals been subjected to verbal and physical abuse by some elements of the community? Deplorably, they have, perhaps even more so in recent years because of the militance of their movement.

Yet the majority of people in America have been courteous and willing to accept homosexuals in their midst, despite the fact that most Americans don't approve of deviant sexual behavior. In fact, in recent years Americans—inundated with propaganda about the genetic or hormonal origins of homosexuality—have allowed state antisodomy laws to be repealed and special "gay rights ordinances" to replace them. And they have done so largely because they have been led to believe that the old laws were unfair to people who were "born that way".

Of course the homosexual community has increased its attacks on the nation with each new victory, charging that persecution is at an all-time high, that "hate attacks" are on the increase, that "homophobia" is the most pressing problem in American society. Their agenda becomes more outrageous with each new victory; their cries become more frenzied, their group behavior more hostile. What we are witnessing is a disease running its course, worsening because it is not being treated.

Therein lies the dilemma for those religious people who genuinely believe in helping their homosexual brothers and sisters. On the one hand, this pathetic segment of our community is in desperate need of love and understanding. On the other hand, they are maddened by the very idea that they are anything but normal and happy. Or, as they put it, they are "gay" but not pathological. So in order to help them, we must first penetrate the rhetorical wall they have built around themselves and then convince them that they are not normal or healthy but actually in need of considerable support.

Many people who feel sympathy for homosexuals try to help by agreeing with what they say about themselves, joining their support groups, contributing money to the National Gay and Lesbian Task Force, and generally condemning anyone who tries to say anything to the contrary. The homosexuals know that there is a great deal of such sentiment in the country at this time, and they shrewdly play to it in their public statements, picturing themselves as victims of the same kind of hatred that Blacks experienced in an earlier time, while unleashing the most malevolent attacks imaginable on those who oppose their political agenda. Thus they appeal to the sense of guilt and moral responsibility that religious people have always felt about the sufferings of those less fortunate.

And thus the Jewish and Christian communities are torn apart over this issue. There seems to be no easy reconciliation of the two sides within the foreseeable future. Currently several of the major Christian denominations are at war with one another over the issue—and in the Episcopal church the issue is in part responsible for talk of a schism—with some of the bishops leaving to form a new body.

So the religious questions raised by homosexuality cannot be ignored in any discussion of the issue. These questions must be confronted in all their complexity and somehow resolved.

Otherwise the nation will lose its soul without ever fully understanding why.

I. What Orthodox People Are Being Asked to Give Up

Those who demand that religious traditionalists change their mind on this particular issue invariably avoid the full implications of what they are asking. "Simply recognize the right of gay people to express their own sexuality", they say. "Simply put aside your old prejudices against such conduct and get in tune with the spirit of the age, which is more and more non-judgmental where sex is concerned. Simply quit being 'old-fashioned'."

But the decision really isn't as "simple" as the liberals make it. In order to accept homosexual behavior as permissible in a Judeo-Christian community, traditionalists would have to renounce or ignore several of the most important assumptions about their Faith—for many *the* most important. In a sense to ask us to "get in tune with the spirit of the age" is the equivalent of asking a physicist to abandon the idea of cause and effect or a geometrician to reject the old-fashioned notion that *pi* is 3.14159265. . . . It is these "old-fashioned notions" on which the very practice of physics and geometry is based. Likewise, there are certain notions on which the very practice of the Christian Faith is based. Several of these are challenged by the homosexual activists, among them the following:

A. BIBLICAL AUTHORITY

Virtually all orthodox Jews and Christians believe in scriptural authority as the foundation of their Faith. Jews live by the Law and by the Talmud, a collection of rabbinical writings. Some Christians believe that only portions of Scripture are to be taken as prescriptive, while others believe that the entire Bible is literally true. But Christian traditionalists tend to unite in a common affirmation that the Gospels are grounded in fact, that the New Testament is prefigured by the Old Testament, and that the moral vision revealed in both is divinely inspired. To believe that the Bible could err in its definition of morality would be to abandon the ultimate source of faith for these orthodox believers. "Once you say that the Bible is wrong about sodomy," they point out, "then you can argue that it is wrong about everything else." Better to believe it all, including the clear statement in both the Old and the New Testaments that sodomy is "a grievous sin".

In case anyone has forgotten just how clear this statement is, let me cite a few of the key passages from the Bible:

> You shall not lie with a male as with a woman; it is an abomination (Lev 18:22).

> Their women exchanged natural relations for unnatural, and the men likewise gave up natural relations with women and were consumed with passion for one another, men committing shameless acts with men and receiving in their own persons the due penalty for their error (Rom 1:27).

> Do not be deceived; neither the immoral, nor idolaters; nor adulterers, nor homosexuals, nor thieves, nor the greedy, nor drunkards, nor revilers, nor robbers will inherit the kingdom of God. And such were some of you. But you were washed, you were sanctified, you were justified in the name of the Lord Jesus Christ and in the Spirit of our God (1 Cor 6:9–11).

> Now we know that the law is good, if any one uses it lawfully, understanding this, that the law is not laid down for the just but for the lawless and disobedient, for the ungodly and sinners, for the unholy and profane, for murderers of fathers and murderers of mothers, for manslayers, immoral persons, sodomites, kidnappers, liars, perjurers and whatever else is contrary to sound doctrine, in accordance with the glorious gospel of the blessed God with which I have been entrusted (1 Tim 1:8–11).

And the angels that did not keep their own position but left their proper dwelling have been kept by him in eternal chains in the nether gloom until the judgment of the great day; just as Sodom and Gomorrah and the surrounding cities, which likewise acted immorally and indulged in unnatural lust, serve as an example by undergoing a punishment of eternal fire (Jude 1:6–7).

These statements are fairly explicit, and there are others that are implicit denunciations of the practice of homosexuality, particularly the Old Testament narrative of Sodom and Gomorrah and the allusion to that narrative in Isaiah. So what should a Bible-grounded Jew or Christian do with such prescriptions? Simply toss them out? If so, what about the rest of the Law or the New Testament? For instance, what should a Christian think about the other sins on Paul's list in 1 Corinthians and 1 Timothy? Are we to believe that idolatry, robbery, matricide, patricide, kidnaping, and perjury are now permissible? If not, then how do we make distinctions? On the basis of current opinion in secular society?

You see, once you begin to be selective about which moral prescriptions you obey and which you dismiss then you are no longer using the Bible as your standard of behavior but are relying on some other authority—and to many religious people, that is the equivalent of saying that someone else has become your god (perhaps even you, yourself).

In an attempt to resolve this dilemma, apologists for homosexuality have suggested that only the words of Jesus can be viewed as absolutely prescriptive, and Jesus said nothing about homosexuality. But He did say: "Think not that I have come to abolish the law and the prophets; I have come not to abolish them but to fulfill them. For truly I say to you, till heaven and earth pass away, not an iota, not a dot will pass from the law until it is all accomplished" (Mt 5:17–18).

As illustrated in the passage from Leviticus, the Law forbids sodomy. Obviously this passage is open to a variety of interpretations, and some will point out obscure segments of the law in Leviticus and Deuteronomy that we no longer credit or observe. But orthodox believers will reply that we should try to obey as much of the Law as we can, particularly when we are given guidance by such New Testament authorities as Paul. To do anything else, they argue, would be to fall into the kind of cultural relativism that was obviously fashionable in Sodom and is fashionable again today.

"Using Scripture selectively", they repeat, "means discarding the Bible as your ultimate authority for belief and action."

B. THE AUTHORITY OF THE HISTORICAL CHURCH

Among Christians, there is a second authority to which many traditionalists look for guidance — the Church. While evangelical Christians tend to rely on Scripture, believers in the Catholic Tradition argue that the ultimate source of all knowledge about God, including the meaning of the Bible, is the historical Church. These people do not reject scriptural authority, but they point out that the Church originally decided which books would be included in Holy Scripture. They also note that the Church has traditionally told us which Old Testament moral strictures are to be taken seriously and which are to be discarded as peculiarly applicable to early times. They admit that from time to time the Church may have fallen into temporal corruption, but they still maintain that what the Church "has always taught" is what we are to believe. And the Church has always taught that homosexual behavior is sinful and contrary to the Will of God.

From this point of view they come to the same conclusions that the evangelicals come to: homosexuality is an abomination. It must not be regarded as either "good" or "normal". And if liberal Christians want to argue that at such and such a time some church tolerated homosexuality, believers in the Catholic tradition will say that "from time to time some individual or groups may have deviated from common teaching, but we must look at the broad sweep of Church history. When we do, sexual promiscuity of all kinds is clearly forbidden. We cannot reject two thousand years of Church teaching for the recent opinions of a contemporary clergy both ignorant of history and disrespectful of authority."

C. FREE WILL

The doctrine of free will is one of the thorniest theological problems posed by belief in God. I will not attempt to define its tortuous paradoxes. I will simply say that most Jews and Christians believe in moral freedom and hold men accountable for their behavior, despite the fact that only God can judge the degree of culpability. Traditionalists reject the modern idea that men are no more than a bundle of automatic responses to external stimuli. Environmental determinism is an idea incompatible with the doctrine that men are made in the image of God. God has a will. So do we. We are therefore responsible for what we do.

This assumption lies at the heart of the religious vision of life, its call for self-renunciation, its prescription of a loving concern for our brothers and sisters. The two go together. If you don't restrain your appetites, then you won't shelter the homeless, clothe the naked, or feed the starving. And if you are merely a product of heredity and environment, then you can't be blamed if you don't. Many proponents of the social gospel are uncomfortable with the idea that we are not moral beings. And certainly traditionalists reject determinism categorically.

Yet in recent times homosexuals have argued with great success that their behavior is the result of tendencies that are inborn and irresistible. They claim their behavior is beyond their control. They cannot do otherwise. They are as instinctive in their sexuality as dogs or worms. Therefore it is wrong-headed and even wicked to require that they adhere to a traditional morality.

Liberal Jews and Christians have been quick to accept this idea without examining its full implications, seeing it, perhaps, as justification for the tolerance of a behavior they are politically disposed to sanction. But the rest of us see the dangers in admitting that any sexual activity can be regarded as socially or morally proper because it is somehow irrepressible. Better to say what traditionalists have always said: "People are responsible for their actions. We can judge those actions. Only God can judge people."

So in the final analysis, we cannot simply consider homosexuality apart from the larger issue of moral authority and individual responsibility. To touch this one question is to disturb the entire fabric of religious thought. We are being asked to surrender too much on the basis of spare evidence and ideological zeal. In the final analysis, orthodox believers must conclude that society may eventually tolerate and even accept homosexual behavior, but only after it has ceased to be religious in any meaningful sense of the word.

II. Homosexuals and the Established Churches

Because of a strong liberal bias in the clergy of most mainline churches, many homosexuals who have "come out" choose to remain a part of the religious bodies into which they were born, sometimes with the approval of the hierarchy, sometimes without it. In fact, there are well-organized homosexual groups operating within most mainline churches. Members of these groups seem to feel a special sense of responsibility to carry on the battle for "gay rights" within the structure of these denominations, often confronting those who oppose them, demanding that old doctrines be set aside in the name of a new, scientifically justified sexual license.

The response to these groups has varied, depending on the nature and structure of the respective church bodies.

Dignity

Perhaps the most visible group among Christians is "Dignity", an organization composed of homosexuals who consider themselves Roman Catholics. Its members have made their presence known throughout the U.S. though they seem to number no more than a few thousand. Dignity's high visibility is in part the consequence of Pope John Paul II's clear reiteration of the historic Catholic position on sexuality outside of marriage and the homosexual organization's militant defiance of the Pope's intransigence. The bold activism of Dignity has received support from some American Catholic clergy who have themselves begun to criticize the ancient biblical prohibitions against homosexuality and sex outside of marriage, as well as the Church's traditional requirement of celibacy for the clergy.

For a while Dignity met and held monthly services in sympathetic Catholic parishes throughout the nation. However, the Vatican has ruled that Church facilities should not be used for homosexual meetings and services, and one by one dioceses have forbidden Dignity meetings on Church property, forcing the group to seek alternative sites. (In Atlanta, for example, they began to meet at the Unitarian Universalist Association facilities.) One newsletter reported that at the end of 1987 there were thirteen chapters of Dignity nationwide.

Dignity has tended to protest the Vatican's unwillingness to approve their sexual behavior in at least two ways: (1) they have spoken out and demonstrated within the established Church structure; and (2) they have established their own "para-church" within which they continue to celebrate the Mass, hold various kinds of "parochial" activities (counseling, prayer groups, instruction), and plan their assaults on the Church hierarchy.

The protest activities of Dignity have been particularly noteworthy at St. Patrick's Cathedral in New York, not only because the city has the largest concentration of homosexual Catholics but also because Cardinal John O'Connor of the Archdiocese of New York has probably been the most forceful opponent of sexual deviance among American Catholics.

Among its protest activities at St. Patrick's, Dignity sponsors a monthly "stand-in" during the sermon. Members stand during the entire homily with their backs to the pulpit, and at one time they even shouted out obscenities, according to a spokesman for the Archdiocese. In December of 1987, eleven members of Dignity were arrested at the cathedral for violating a restraining order issued by the courts at the request of the Archdiocese. Later the charges were dropped.

Also, on St. Valentine's Day 1988, homosexual lovers, both male and female, held a "kiss-in" on the cathedral steps, while the press took pictures that were in turn printed throughout the nation. Dignity justifies such behavior by arguing that the Catholic Church will only be moved to change its mind by such shock tactics.

Dignity's own para-church activities include the sponsorship of such events as a "Come out for Christmas" service for the San Francisco homosexual community and a national convention every two years. In 1987 the site was Miami Beach, where they were joined by delegates to the Metropolitan Community Church convention, an exclusively homosexual denomination (see below).

In 1987 Dignity also issued its "Pastoral Letter on Sexual Ethics", a document intended as a response to official Vatican statements on the subject of homosexuality. Among other things, it said:

> We overwhelmingly disagree with the official Church position that we should abstain from sexual activity. We see our sexuality and its expression as neither handicap nor sin but the holy gift of God. We know from our experience that it is possible to go beyond prohibition and condemnation to bring our spirituality and sexuality together and to express our Christian faith in our sexual lives. . . . We want the way we image God's love to

become clearer. But we know from our experience that God does not automatically give the gift of celibacy together with the gift of homosexuality, and we are convinced that lifelong sexual abstinence is not the only acceptable lifestyle available to the gay and lesbian People of God.[1]

In addition, Sister Jeannine Gamick, at Dignity's tenth anniversary celebration dinner, told of having a "dream" in which Moses came down from the mountain bringing "ten new lesbian/gay commandments". They are as follows:

1. Thou shalt not take the Pope too seriously; this is popolatry.
2. Thou shalt not allow others to take thy name of DIGNITY in vain.
3. Remember to make holy the people, for bishops were meant to serve people, not people to serve bishops.
4. Honor thy foremothers and forefathers who have worked for thee in the lesbian/gay movement.
5. Thou shalt not kill an adult Christian faith by failing to follow thine own convictions.
6. Thou shalt not allow official Church teachings on sexuality to separate thee from the love of thy God.
7. Thou shalt not rob thyself of the love and respect thou deservest.
8. Thou shalt not bear false witness against thine own authority, but learn to trust God's spirit within thee.
9. Thou shalt not covet the smells and bells of the pre-Vatican II Church with its lack of freedom to dissent.
10. Thou shalt not take thyself too seriously, but laugh, climb trees, and smell flowers, because thy God loveth thee very, very much.[2]

---

[1] Dignity, "Pastoral Letter on Sexual Ethics: A Preliminary Study Document Prepared by the Dignity Task Force on Sexual Ethics" (1987): 6–7.
[2] Sister Jeannine Gamick, "Sister Jeannine's Ten C's", in *Calendar: A Publication of Dignity/New York, Inc.* 14 (Feb. 1988): 2, 4.

Integrity

"Integrity" is an organization for homosexual Episcopalians, which, though modeled on Dignity, is far less visible on the national scene, in part because the hierarchy of the Episcopal church has been more receptive to the demands of the homosexual movement than has the Vatican. The presiding bishop, Edmund Browning, does not have the same authority among Episcopalians that the Pope has among Catholics, but he has been viewed by some fellow churchmen as generally sympathetic to the cause of "gay rights". Indeed, he said at the 1988 General Convention in Detroit that the threat of schism, growing in part out of conservative dissatisfaction over sexual issues, was a sign of the Episcopal church's "progress".

More outspoken is Bishop Spong of New Jersey, who has advocated that the church bless "committed" homosexuals who enter into sexual liaisons. Spong, who has compared such a ceremony to the blessing of a hunt, is the leader of a strong and active prohomosexual faction within the House of Bishops who do much of Integrity's work within the church hierarchy. In his most recent book, *Living in Sin?* the bishop has affirmed the goodness of homosexual unions, maintained that homosexual proclivities are hereditary and therefore "natural", and proposed that the church bless homosexual unions. He even offers a sample liturgy for such a ceremony.

Integrity itself is an active lobbying force within the Episcopal church, with chapters in virtually every major city in the United States, including New York, Philadelphia, Washington, Miami, Dallas, St. Louis, San Francisco, San Diego, Boston, Cleveland, and Denver.

Other Denominations

Homosexual organizations in other faiths do exist, although as the hierarchical structure of the religious body becomes less centralized, the necessity of a separate and active organization of homosexuals becomes less and less obvious. For example, the city of New York is officially in liaison with a number of such groups, including the following: Affirmation–United Methodists for Gay and Lesbian Concerns, Conference for Catholic Lesbians, Evangelicals Concerned, Friends for Lesbian and Gay Concerns (Gay Quakers), Seventh Day Adventists (Kinship), Unitarian Universalists for Lesbian and Gay Concerns, Lutherans for Lesbian and Gay Concerns, and United Church of Christ Coalition for Lesbian and Gay Concerns.

Some homosexuals, however, prefer a church of their own, and one has indeed been established.

III. The Homosexual Church

The Reverend Troy Perry is founder of the Universal Fellowship of Metropolitan Community Churches (UFMCC or MCC)—a homosexual denomination that by the middle of 1987 numbered 267 congregations worldwide, though the total membership was estimated at fewer than 35,000. In a very real sense Perry is a "primate", and his church is one of the fastest growing denominations in America. UFMCC is for homosexuals and holds that sexual relations between persons of the same sex are highly desirable, with a few broad exceptions.

For example, UFMCC believes adultery is a sin, but the meaning of the word changes in the altered circumstances of Perry's word. As he explains it: "That's the breaking of vows you make to another human being. If you have an open relationship and you're honest about that and you've both agreed to that, that's fine and dandy. If you don't and you lie about it and run around . . . then you're as bad as our enemies."[3]

---

[3] Troy Perry, quoted in *Dallas Voice* (July 19, 1989), 24.

Perry also defines three other areas of sexual sin that he has preached against since he started his church in Los Angeles in 1968:

> Number one was, I believe that rape is a sin. I believe forcing yourself on someone who doesn't want your attention is absolutely wrong. The second one was, I had problems with people who would go out . . . in broad daylight and have intercourse in the street. . . . I've always felt that was not appropriate.
> The third area was sex with children. I have problems with adults who go to bed with seven-, eight- and nine-year-old kids; I just do.[4]

Perry's personal opinions provide most of the theological authority for his sermons and social gospel. For example, he has advised members of his church not to take the HIV test: "I've refused to take the test. I tell all of my friends, I'll take the test the day they have the treatment. . . . I just encourage my friends not to do it. They don't need that extra stress in their lives."[5]

But what about the possibility of exposing others to the virus? Doesn't he think that each individual has the responsibility to learn whether or not he is infected so that he can avoid passing the disease along to those who are AIDS free? Perry has an answer: "I presume we've all been exposed to the virus. I just take the attitude every gay man has been exposed to the virus, but I refuse to go down there and have my name in some computer somewhere. They will drag me away to give me any kind of test."[6]

Perry's influence is substantial in California, where stringent laws have been passed in response to homosexual fears about AIDS. In fact, Perry claims that MCC is influential around the globe:

> We're now the largest organization touching the lives of gays and lesbians in the world. There is no organization larger than MCC—nowhere else. We've researched this to death. There are groups that receive more money from federal funding and

[4] Ibid.
[5] Ibid.
[6] Ibid.

things like that, but on a basis of people contributing to an organization we're now raising more money than anybody. Our membership is contributing approximately $6 million a year now.[7]

Perry began his denomination in Huntington Park, California, in 1968; his first "church building" was the living room of his apartment. A father of two who "came out of the closet", he was living with a male lover when, "called to the ministry", he placed an advertisement in the *Advocate* for anyone interested in joining a homosexual church. He had thirteen people at his first service, and from that time forward UFMCC has been growing, while several of the mainline churches have been declining in membership.

Perry has been an activist since the late sixties and has led a number of "gay rights" demonstrations. He has also fasted in order to gain public support for his issues. His longest fast was for sixteen days in 1978, when he was trying to raise money to combat the "Briggs Initiative".[8] As he explains it:

> I announced that I wouldn't eat again until I raised $100,000 seed money. . . . The Lord had spoke to my heart and told me this was a *real* moral issue, not the way John Briggs and Anita Bryant were trying to portray it, and let me know what I was to do. . . . On the sixteenth day of my fast—of just drinking water for 16 days—we went over the top with $104,000.[9]

When someone suggested that this technique sounded suspiciously like Oral Roberts' much-criticized "God will call me home" appeal, Perry was quick to point out what he considered significant differences:

> I said this is a matter of morals. I said, people have to know how serious we are, we who are a part of the gay and lesbian community. I refuse to eat again. If it means my death, it means my death.

---

[7] Ibid., 27.
[8] Refers to Senator John Briggs, a California state senator who became associated with a referendum to make it illegal in that state to employ in the public schools persons who "engaged in advocating, soliciting, imposing, encouraging, or promoting private or public homosexual acts".
[9] Perry, quoted in *Dallas Voice* (July 12, 1989), 25.

That's not the way Oral did it. Mr. Roberts said God told him "I'll *kill* you if you don't raise this money." God didn't tell me that. . . . This was my offering. . . . I knew I would receive the money. I didn't know how long it would take, but I knew with all my heart that the gay community and our heterosexual friends would respond.[10]

And many heterosexuals did respond. The *Dallas Voice*, a homosexual newspaper, reported that "Abigail Van Buren and Jane Fonda were among the 'Friends of Troy Perry' who took out full-page ads encouraging donations".[11]

In addition to "Dear Abby" and Jane Fonda, Perry also speaks highly of Phil Donohue:

He and I know each other quite well. He and his wife, Marlo Thomas, are recipients of our Human Rights award from MCC this year, and will be in Miami to receive the award on Saturday, July 25 [1987]. We feel like they have done more for gay rights— in the media—than any person. They've never backed away from the issue and have always been extremely positive.[12]

Perry was also a key figure in organizing the National March on October 11 of 1987, in which some 200,000 homosexuals participated. In speaking of the event beforehand, he said:

I feel like we've *got* to get to Washington, D.C. It is time for us to have a much more visible march than we had the last time. I'm the one who penned the phrase, "For love and for life, we're not going back." I based it on a scripture, "Our God, who has given us life, also gives us liberty."

The day the Supreme Court ruled that we didn't have any rights, that the states could do anything they wanted to us against us, I was never so irritated in my life. That's when I said, "It is now time for another massive demonstration, America." And I found there were other people feeling just the way I was.[13]

In July of 1987 UFMCC and Dignity, a homosexual organization, held a joint convention in Miami Beach attended by

[10] Ibid.
[11] Ibid.
[12] Ibid.
[13] Ibid.

some 1,500 delegates. According to the *Advocate:* "Six years in the planning, the historic occasion included an evening of joint activities—worship service, dinner, poolside disco and entertainment by New York Jewish leather lesbian Lynn Lavner."[14]

IV. The Religious Dilemma

Let me paraphrase the argument the homosexual community is making in its assault on the Christian community. While what I say will be simpler and more straightforward than the usual statements made by homosexual leaders, I submit that I am not exaggerating either the message we are receiving or the rhetoric in which it is couched. This, then, is that message:

"We, the homosexual population, are now convinced from the few studies that support the claim that our sexual orientation is the product of hereditary factors. Homosexuality, therefore, is a natural condition—i.e., one produced by nature—and as such was created by God (if there *is* a God) and therefore is good. As a matter of fact, not only is homosexuality no more than an 'alternate life-style', it is also equal to heterosexuality and should be so regarded by Christians and Jews.

"As for the Bible, much of what is written there is the product of ignorance and primitive superstition. The Jewish prohibition against 'sodomy' was instituted because of tribal needs for more progeny. (Homosexuals did not produce children.) The Apostle Paul, who spoke against homosexuality with particular emphasis, was at the very least influenced by the idea that Christ would be returning any day and that sexual involvement would therefore detract from spiritual preparations. Then, too, Paul himself seemed to have had some hangups, and his homophobia may have been evidence of repressed homosexual feelings on his part—the 'thorn in his flesh'.

[14] Steve Warren, *Advocate* (Sept. 1, 1987), 30.

"As for Jesus, He never said a word of condemnation against homosexuality, a fact that indicates that He didn't really see anything wrong with such attachments.

"Relying on these isolated statements in the Bible, as well as an ongoing tradition of bigotry, Jews and Christians have been homophobes for the better part of 3,000 years, persecuting homosexuals more than any other minority in the history of Western civilization.

"But now the tide has turned. We have at last 'come out', and in so doing we have exposed the mean-spirited nature of Judeo-Christian morality. You have been narrow-minded and self-righteous. But with the help of a growing number of your own membership, we are going to force you to recant everything you have ever believed or said about sexuality. Here are some of the things you will be expected to affirm, in the process of renouncing love, marriage, and family:

1. Henceforth homosexuality will be spoken of in your churches and synagogues as an 'honorable estate'.

2. You can either let us marry people of the same sex or better yet abolish marriage altogether, since it will give the lie to everything you have said and done in the past about sexuality.

3. You will also be expected to offer ceremonies that bless our sexual arrangements, whether or not you retain marriage as something to be celebrated in your churches.

4. You will also instruct your young people in homosexual as well as heterosexual behavior, and you will go out of your way to make certain that homosexual youths are allowed to date, attend religious functions together, openly display affection, and enjoy each other's sexuality without embarrassment or guilt.

5. If any of the older people in your midst object, you will deal with them sternly, making certain they renounce their ugly and ignorant homophobia or suffer public humiliation.

6. You will also make certain that all of the prestige and resources of your institutions are brought to bear on the community, so that laws are passed forbidding discrimination

against homosexuals and heavy punishments are assessed. We expect and demand the same commitment to us that you made to Blacks and to women, though their suffering has not been as great as ours.

7. Finally, we will in all likelihood want to expunge a number of passages from your Scriptures and rewrite others, eliminating preferential treatment of marriage and using words that will allow for homosexual interpretations of passages describing biblical lovers such as Ruth and Boaz or Solomon and the Queen of Sheba.

"Warning: If all of these things do not come to pass quickly, we will subject orthodox Jews and Christians to the most sustained hatred and vilification in recent memory. We have captured the liberal establishment and the press. We have already beaten you on a number of battlefields. And we have the spirit of the age on our side. You have neither the faith nor the strength to fight us, so you might as well surrender now."

Are those of us who believe in traditional religious values really caught on the horns of this dilemma? Do we have to renounce the beliefs and scriptural authority of 3,000 years because the spirit of the age demands that we do? Many religious and Church leaders are telling us we must, and it is difficult to argue with them because their voices sound so reasonable and authoritative.

But such is always the case when the world speaks to us, asking us to give up our faith and do what is fashionable and pragmatic and easy. The Jews were asked to give up a religion of self-discipline and worship Baal. How much easier it was for those who did. The Baalites went up to "the high places", got drunk, and had an orgy. They must have called the Jews who refused to join them "narrow-minded" and "prudish" and "puritanical". They still do.

The Christians who lived among the Nazis were asked to hate the Jews and to give their ultimate allegiance to Hitler's vulgar dream of a secular millennium. Some of them, like

Dietrich Bonhoeffer, preferred to die. How much easier it would have been had he just made the compromises necessary to live comfortably within the Third Reich and to accept the alterations in the Ten Commandments that the Fuhrer demanded. We are still being asked to modify those Commandments.

In many ways the choice we are being offered is subtler and therefore more difficult to refuse. Instead of asking us to give up our God in favor of another, or in favor of the state, we are now being asked to believe in the same God—only one who has now changed His mind about things He once said.

Or else we must simply admit that the Scriptures are not only not literally true but also subject to complete revision in the light of changing political currents. Since the Old Testament prophets and New Testament disciples didn't understand the remarkable revelation about human sexuality that has come to us in the past twenty years, we must view everything they said as suspect, testing it against the slogans of the National Organization of Women and the National Gay and Lesbian Task Force.

The voices of the secular world would be more credible if they could say that what they are offering is "science" rather than "revelation". Most of us believe that nothing that God tells us can really be contrary to facts of the physical universe He created. So we are never required to reject scientific fact in order to stay in communion with God.

But—as I have already suggested in Chapter One—there is no question of the facts being denied, not in the matter of homosexuality. What we are dealing with is not fact but ideology, not science but opinion, not truth but empty rhetoric. We are being asked to give up our Judeo-Christian heritage for a few bumper sticker platitudes.

Let's look at those platitudes and see what really lies behind them.

"God loves gay people too"

Of course He does. Just as much as He loves all the rest of us. No orthodox Jew or Christian argues otherwise. And by the way, He loves murderers and racists and wife-beaters and self-righteous Pharisees, just as much as He loves homosexuals—no less. But the fact that God loves us has nothing to do with whether or not He approves of the way we behave. We all behave badly, each in a different way; and God disapproves of many things we do, but His love isn't conditional on our good behavior—nor should ours be for one another. We must love one another despite our bad behavior—and anyone who says "God loves gay people too", with the implication that God therefore approves of their "life-style", doesn't know Who God is or—for that matter, what love is.

"Jesus never said a word against homosexuality"

Many homosexuals point to this omission as proof that Jesus didn't disapprove of homosexual practices. Jesus didn't mention rape either. Or child molesting. Or bestiality. Or arson. Or many of the crimes that are unanimously condemned by society—His as well as ours. In all likelihood He didn't mention them because He didn't think He needed to. All of those crimes—including homosexuality—were too obviously transgressions against the Law—and among the rarer ones. He did condemn fornication—that is, sex outside of marriage—because it was a more commonplace sin and therefore one in need of specific mention. Was it necessary to note as well that sodomy was also sex outside of marriage?

"The Church has always taught that sex is sinful"

Never in the Church's long history have Jews and Christians taught anything of the sort. People who say the contrary are ignorant or else they misunderstand the history of the Faith. In the Jewish world in which Christ lived, marriage was a *religious* rite, one that blessed the sexual union of a man and woman. The fact that marriages are performed in churches and have been for centuries is ample proof that the Christian Church blesses the sexual union of a man and woman who intend to spend a lifetime together. When those who attack the

Church as "puritanical" cite the celibacy of the Catholic clergy, it is because they fail to make a distinction between the sacrifices asked of those who make a special commitment to God and those who lead ordinary lives. Priests and nuns in the Catholic Church also give up worldly possessions, but that doesn't mean the Church thinks houses and automobiles are wicked.

"We know a lot more about sexuality today and therefore can make new rules"

The "new" things we know about sex are not things that change the basic problems that sexual promiscuity inevitably causes. In part Jews and Christians believe in sexual fidelity because they believe in families. The presence of a father and mother during the formative years of a child clearly makes an enormous difference in how he turns out. If common sense didn't tell us that in earlier times, statistics now make it undeniable. (The incidence of unwanted pregnancy among teenagers, for example, is significantly reduced when a girl grows up with her natural parents present in the household.) In addition, there is something about the relationship between parents and children that teaches us about the relationship of men to God. Certainly it is easier to understand how God could love even the worst of us if we have had children of our own—and that is an important lesson to religious people, more important than the sense of freedom that some single people claim to feel. Then, too, in a genuinely monogamous marriage, there is a sense of belonging to one another in a way that would preclude the inclusion of any third party. These are matters that Dr. Ruth neither understands nor believes in, nor have they been altered by the advance in birth control techniques or the latest hormonal study.

"Homosexual relations in youth help us to understand more fully the nature of our own sexuality"

This idea, expressed by such sexologists as Deryck Calderwood, is virtually without meaning. As soon as you ask experts to explain just *how* you discover what it means to be "male" by having sex with other men or "female" by having sex with other women, they begin to use vague and circumlocutious language and finally end up talking nonsense. If you don't understand the "nature of your own sexuality"—and most people past the age of twelve do—then probably the most confusing thing you could do would be to enter into a physical relationship with someone of your own sex. Men and women learn best about their own sexuality by getting married and taking a lifetime to explore the meaning of genuine love as God intended us to know and understand it.

"How can you presume to judge other people?"

You can't. Only God can judge other people. But we are required to judge acts and to say they are good or bad—quite apart from the person who commits them. We can no more judge a homosexual than we can judge the leader of a lynch mob, but we can say that lynching is wrong—and if we can say that, then we have a right to say that sodomy is wrong as well, and for more than one reason. Everyone judges the actions of others; the trick is to say after having done so: "Still, he may well be a better human than I am." See if those who preach tolerance of all kinds of sexual behavior can be nonjudgmental about "homophobia".

V. What Can Religious People Do about Homosexuality?

What is the proper religious response to homosexuality and its most dangerous by-product, AIDS? No question is more in need of immediate and authoritative response. On the one hand, homosexuals and their allies are demanding that the Judeo-Christian condemnation of homosexual acts be renounced in the face of "new and conclusive medical evidence", while, on the other hand, some antihomosexual extremists are calling for the exile of all AIDS patients to some equivalent of a desert island. Clearly the religious community must respond to the growing militance of the homosexual movement and to the rampant disease that this militance inevitably has generated. But how?

First, I think we must prove that we truly believe in the tenets of our Faith by extending a helping hand to the homosexual community. Our most immediate priority in this regard must be the assistance of AIDS victims, a growing number of suffering men and women who have enormous physical and emotional needs. Instead of spending a billion dollars on educating the nation about condoms, we should be concentrating more of our attention on caring for the sick and the dying. We need more medical research, more AZT at a lower cost, more testing and treatment facilities, more hospital beds for AIDS patients, more hospices, more counseling for the dying.

Even if the more frightening projections prove to be inaccurate, the nation is still facing a traumatic decade of death and sorrow, with which the influenza epidemic of 1918 and the polio outbreaks of the 1940s will pale by comparison. The deaths will be greater in number, and the guilt and recriminations will be overpowering. We must begin to prepare ourselves for this day by learning to forgive one another and help one another—now, while it is still relatively easy to do so. Virtue is more habit than inspiration, and we must cultivate the virtue of charity against a time when the natural reactions will be fear and anger.

Our churches need to speak to these issues now, and they need to do so without reference to current public policy. Too many liberal clergy pay lip service to compassion while pushing a political agenda that furthers the sexual revolution. They are not interested in comforting the afflicted so much as in altering traditional attitudes toward promiscuity and perversion. Let those churches who say they want to show compassion for AIDS victims spend their resources on direct care rather than on propaganda. Let them volunteer for hospitals and hospices rather than demonstrate in front of the White House. Let them take the burden on their own shoulders rather than shift it to government. When Jesus saw hungry people on the mountainside, He fed them. He didn't make a speech denouncing Caesar's lack of compassion.

At the same time, our orthodox religious bodies must address the larger problem of homosexuality in a positive and charitable way, not denouncing the wickedness of sinners so much as providing ways for them to amend their lives. Whether homosexuality is a psychological illness, a disorder of the spirit, a failure of the will, or all of these things, it *can* be cured; yet thus far too many traditional-minded people have ignored this fact, preferring to put the whole matter of sexual perversion into a dark closet, only to remember it when they open the door by mistake.

But a few ministries are in the field, and they are making a difference in bringing redemption to the lives of men and women who have been courageous enough to ask for help. Among these are the following:

Regeneration

Located in Baltimore, Maryland. Director Alan Medinger describes one of his several groups as follows: "The typical man in this group is about thirty years old. He never chose to be homosexual, but he has struggled with the condition for much of his life. He is a Christian and has been for a number of years. He's been involved with Regeneration for between six months and two years. There is a way in which he is in a no-man's-land or a desert. He has left Egypt behind, but the promised land seems so far off."[15]

Yet the promised land is indeed attainable. Medinger himself has arrived there after his own years in the desert, and he reports that many more have made it as well—either leading

---

[15] Alan Medinger, "Regeneration News" (May 1988): 2.

lives of satisfying restraint or else married and even the parents of children, as is Medinger.

He has begun to organize groups up and down the east coast, but he reports the progress is slow. His own denomination—the Episcopal church—has been largely uncooperative and even hostile, though individual parishes have offered their help and facilities. The evangelicals, he says, are sympathetic but prefer not to address the issue at all.

White Stone Ministries

Located in Boston, this group has an office at Ruggles Baptist church, where counselors Mike Mitchel and Linda Frank work with both men and women who want to change their sexual habits.

Mitchel is convinced that people are not born irrevocably homosexual. "I went through it and I've gotten through it, and God's healing me. So if you've got the desire, it'll happen—you'll change", he says. Linda Frank agrees: "The fact is, if I really was gay (which I really was), and I really have changed (which I really have), then that puts the responsibility on them . . . no longer can they use the excuse 'I was born this way'. They then have to reckon with the fact that, well, maybe it is possible to change."[16]

Desert Stream Ministries

This group, one of the better known "ex-gay" ministries, is located in Santa Monica, California. Its director, Andy Comiskey, says of his program: "We're becoming a lot wiser. As we've worked with more people and learned from our mistakes as well as our victories, I think we're better able now to actually facilitate the healing process."[17]

Comiskey estimates that out of ten people who inquire at his ministry, six will come to a meeting, four will commit to a

[16] *Christian Science Monitor* (Mar. 3, 1988).
[17] Ibid.

"year-long program of prayer, psychological counseling, and study entitled 'Sexual Redemption in Christ'. Three out of those four are ultimately successful in putting their homosexuality behind them."[18]

When asked if his program really works, Comiskey, an ex-homosexual who is now married, says: "It definitely works. I live with the result of it all the time in my own life."

L.I.F.E.

Run by Ron and Joanne Highley, L.I.F.E. is located in New York City and more than many of the other ministries is biblically centered. The group publishes testimonials, accounts of marriages growing out of cures, and photographs of subsequent children.

In explaining why homosexuals have difficulty coping with their problems, a L.I.F.E. brochure says:

> When an adult says he has been homosexual all his life (therefore "born that way"), he is recalling his emotional state from his earliest remembrance and accepting an identity that distorts the truth about God, others, and himself. In reaction to rejection or trauma, the child will unconsciously detach the mind from the emotions as a protective mechanism. The mind retreats into a fantasy world apart from reality and authority. Protection from further hurt becomes all important, and confrontation or dealing with problems is avoided; the mind may become passive, the will rebellious, and the emotions dominant. The afflictions of the child then become the sins in the adult, who must repent, forgive, and come to know God as his Father, Healer, Protector.
> It is the responsibility of God's people to tell the truth in love: that God wants to heal the wounds and forgive the sins that have blinded us to His design and purpose for us.[19]

Courage

This organization founded by Fr. John F. Harvey of St. Michal's Rectory in New York City. Fr. Harvey, who contin-

[18] Ibid.
[19] L.I.F.E., Inc., "Understanding Homosexuality", unsigned, undated brochure.

ues to guide this service ministry, writes the following about the work of the organization:

> COURAGE is a spiritual support group for Catholic homosexual persons who desire to live a life in accord with the gospel. Having disavowed homosexual activity, the members of the group seek to live a life of celibacy or sexual abstinence from homosexual activity. The members themselves composed the following five purposes:
>
> 1. To live chaste lives in accordance with the Roman Catholic Church's teachings on homosexuality.
> 2. To dedicate our entire lives to Christ through service to others, spiritual reading, prayer, meditation, individual spiritual direction, frequent attendance at Mass and the frequent reception of the sacraments of Penance and of the Holy Eucharist.
> 3. To foster a spirit of fellowship in which we may share with one another our thoughts and experiences and so ensure that none of us will have to face the problems of homosexuality alone.
> 4. To be mindful of the truth that chaste friendships are not only possible but necessary in celibate Christian life and to encourage one another in forming and sustaining them.
> 5. To live lives that may serve as good examples to other homosexuals.
>
> Courage has spread to three foundations in New York City and other foundations throughout the United States and Canada. At the weekly meetings the Twelve Steps of Alcoholics Anonymous are adapted to the homosexual condition. Through prayer and group support individuals have been able to lead a chaste life. For more information people can write to Courage, St. Michael's Rectory, 424 W. 34th St. New York, NY 10001, or telephone (212) 421-0426.[20]

Exodus International

Located in San Rafael, California, this is an umbrella organization for the more than seventy-five "ex-gay ministries

[20] Taken from "Courage: A Handbook" (New York: Courage, 1987), and from a letter from Fr. John Harvey dated May 19, 1989.

worldwide". According to the *Christian Science Monitor*, "It serves as an accrediting body and serves as host of an annual training conference." Andrew Comiskey is its president.[21]

These kinds of programs deserve our moral and financial support. They (and perhaps they alone) are addressing the spiritual problem of homosexuality in American society. Religious bodies that either turn their backs on homosexuals or else encourage them in their delusions are failing to serve God as fully and completely as they might. Homosexual ministries must increase in size and popular support if they are ever to redeem the neglect of these sad and confused people who are now so troublesome to us.

To summarize, we must hold out the hand of fellowship to homosexuals, but we cannot compromise in our condemnation of homosexual acts. We must continue to remind our liberal friends that there is a crucial distinction between these two things, a distinction that has been lost in much of the public discussion on this issue.

However, we must also remind our conservative friends that they cannot forget that all men are made in the image of God and are equally precious in His sight. While we cannot permit our nation to become a society free of all sexual restraint, we must also avoid becoming a society of Pharisees, forever giving thanks to God that we are not as other men.

I'm not sure which would be worse.

---

[21] *Christian Science Monitor* (Mar. 3, 1988).

CHAPTER FOUR

The Politics of Homosexuality

On June 26, 1988 an event occurred in New York City that would have profoundly disturbed such old-time residents as Alexander Hamilton, Chester A. Arthur, Boss Tweed, Al Smith, Fiorello LaGuardia, and Nelson Rockefeller—though apparently it has not bothered Mario Cuomo, Geraldine Ferraro, or Ed Koch.

I am speaking of the annual New York Gay and Lesbian Pride March.

The event was preceded by a summer rain that drenched the streets for about thirty minutes. Then, around 12:30, it began, and it didn't end for almost two and a half hours. Mostly it was made up of automobiles covered with balloons and gangs of people in shorts carrying signs, but occasionally there was a real float or a group of professional music makers. A chorus of men, for example, sang Broadway show tunes.

It was really a careless ragtag parade, in its best moments no more than a halfhearted imitation of all the other parades that move down Fifth Avenue in a given year. Small wonder that almost nobody watched it, except the shoppers and sightseers who were out on the sidewalks anyway and paused for a minute or two to gaze in bemused curiosity. Of course there were television crews strung out along the route, and they may have been the most numerous nonwalkers on the scene. But it was appropriate that they be there in such large numbers, because the parade was really a media event.

The Gay Pride Parade is an event that is now being repeated in major cities all over the country. As always, the atmosphere was part celebratory, part defiant—a mixture of prancing high jinx and accusatory slogans. There was a float depicting the Pope as a puppet controlled by the devil. Some of the signs were obscene. And in a moment of high solemnity, thousands of balloons with the names of AIDS victims inside were released: a spectacle of color for the cameras to follow into the sky.

As the marchers passed St. Patrick's Cathedral, some turned and jabbed the air with their middle fingers, perhaps as a gesture of contempt for their archenemy Cardinal John O'Connor (who believes in love and forgiveness for homosexuals and AIDS sufferers but refuses to tell them they are normal or guiltless). Or perhaps they were gesturing at the fifteen or so protestors who held up a sign that read: "AIDS is the scourge of God."

Among the groups that marched this year were Dykes and Tykes, Dignity (Catholic homosexuals), the Gay Men's Health Crisis, the National Gay and Lesbian Task Force, and, among them, the North American Man-Boy Love Association (NAMBLA). This last group is composed of pedophiles, or more precisely, of men who like to have sex with very young boys.

In many respects the relatively high profile of NAMBLA defines the progress that homosexuals have made over the past thirty-five years. Had the existence of such a group been known in the 1950s, they would have been hounded out of town or thrown into jail, where they would have been lucky to survive their sentences, since even hardened convicts in earlier times had little patience with child molesters.

Today, however, NAMBLA is a highly visible national organization, though a small one. They put out a newsletter filled with pictures of male children, they hold conventions, and they appear on network television talk shows. Their announced political goal is the elimination or severe alteration of age-of-consent laws, and they argue their case using the rhetoric of the civil rights movement. Little boys, they say, have as much right as adults to engage in consensual sex, and only a repressive society would prevent them from enjoying such exquisite pleasures at the earliest possible age. One international pedophile has popularized the slogan "Sex before Eight, or It's Too Late".

As this bunch ambled along, they were just another segment of the parade, indistinguishable in appearance and in the tone of their rhetoric. They have been at it for a good many years now, and they are making progress. The American Psychiatric Association, following the same path it blazed in "normalizing" homosexuality, has revised its *Diagnostic and Statistical Manual of Psychiatric Disorders* to indicate that pedophilia is now regarded as "normal" under certain circumstances: that is, when the pedophile does not feel guilty after fantasizing about having intercourse with a child. In the wake of this new "scientific discovery", can the reduction of a legal age of consent be far behind? Who in our society today would be so intolerant or so backward as to oppose these men, who were walking past the spires of New York's fashionably liberal churches, grim smiles on their faces, a haunted look in their eyes?

After a rainy start, they all walked in the sunshine; later the *New York Times* spoke about the fun and the pathos, as if this had been the Fighting 69th returning from World War I or the V.J. Day Parade in 1945. And indeed it was a victory parade of sorts, the celebration of an enemy in the process of being conquered, a nation sinking to its knees.

The nation, of course, is the United States of America, which is surrendering to this growing army of revolutionaries without firing a shot, indeed, without more than a word or two of protest. The homosexual blitzkrieg has been better planned and better executed than Hitler's. Unlike the French, who wept in the streets of Paris as the Germans marched by, we don't even know we've been conquered—at least not yet.

In part we are ignorant because we don't understand what a "gay rights parade" really means, while the homosexuals understand all too well. They realize that when they can march down our main thoroughfares, with our official permission and the protection of the police, they have become not a klatch of sexual deviates but a "movement" and therefore constitutionally blessed. Instead of poor lost sheep who need to be brought back into the fold, they are now a political force with a political agenda, and as such they have become one more alternative to the increasingly confused mainstream of American thought.

When homosexuals can march down Fifth Avenue in emulation of the Easter Parade, then they are saying that what happens in their bedrooms and what happened on a Sunday morning 2,000 years ago are in some way equally important, equally valuable, equally legitimate in our society, and it is *legitimacy* above all else that the homosexual movement is now claiming. And they are on the verge of achieving that legitimacy, not just in this century but in this decade.

But how did they come so far so fast in this quest? In order to answer this question, it is necessary to review the history of the movement over the past three decades.

I. The Homosexual Movement: 1960 to the Present

In the 1960s, when antiwar protestors were crowding the streets of the nation, demanding the complete reconstitution of American society, homosexual activists were not an important part of the anarchic coalition. In fact, they were virtually nonexistent. Homosexuals kept a low profile, remaining "in the closet" throughout the decade, largely because their time had not yet arrived.

Dennis Altman, author of *The Homosexualization of America*, describes the climate as follows:

> During my first stay in the United States (1964–1966), when I was beginning to come to terms with my sexuality, homosexuality was both hidden and stigmatized. . . . Until the end of the sixties, to be a homosexual in most Western countries, and especially in the United States, was to experience a life that was largely furtive, shameful, and guilt-ridden; most homosexuals

shared only too strongly the social condemnations against them.
. . . [M]uch of the sixties counterculture was as sexist and
homophobic as the mainstream culture.[1]

But the unrest of the 1960s had set the stage for the late
entrance of the homosexuals to the revolutionary movement.
For the first time in its history, America had come to doubt its
own essential virtue. Having been told by academics, news
commentators, and hippies that it was morally depraved and
endemically unjust, the nation came to a moment of self-
loathing epitomized by the remark of President Jimmy Carter
that Americans were afflicted by a "malaise" of our own making.

At this moment homosexual activists began to emerge from
the shadows to take advantage of society's self-doubt, to reas-
sert the same old charges of corruption, this time in connection
with sexual laws and attitudes. Americans were bigoted,
unjust, and repressive. Homosexuals would stand for it no
longer. They too were now demanding their rights.

Again, Dennis Altman analyzes the situation:

> The seventies saw the beginning of the large-scale transition in
> the status of homosexuality from a deviance or perversion to an
> alternate life style or minority, as remarkable a change in the
> characterization of "the homosexual" as was the original inven-
> tion of that category in the nineteenth century. Along with this
> change, homosexuals were being cast increasingly in the role of
> the vanguard of social and sexual change, worthy of consider-
> able media attention.[2]

The rhetoric of the homosexual movement, which is more
reminiscent of civil rights demonstrators than of antiwar protestors, has obscured the essentially revolutionary nature of
their demands. They are asking for "rights", insisting they are
the victims of "bigotry", demanding that they not be discriminated against because of an accident of birth; yet they are asking for no less than the complete restructuring of American

[1] Altman, 2.
[2] Ibid.

life. Our idea of a society encompasses not merely the idea of marriage as central to a stable community but also the belief in a strong sexual morality. These assumptions have provided continuity to the American experience since the earliest days of the Republic. In order to accommodate the homosexuals, we would have to discard those unquestioned values that have always undergirded the American social order. So far most people have failed to understand the extreme political implications of what is going on.

The homosexuals understand all too well. Dennis Altman makes the point quite explicitly:

> [A]ny affirmation of homosexuality is an attack on the prevalent values. Hence, to declare the validity of homosexuality, to reject the judgment that it is sick, evil, a maladjustment, a deviance, or a perversion, is a political statement, and the assertion of a homosexual identity is as much a political act as was the assertion of a Czech or Romanian identity in the nineteenth century.[3]

By the late 1970s homosexuals were demanding that they be allowed to lead their own lives without interference from government. They were demanding that sodomy laws be abolished, that people quit characterizing them as either morally lax or mentally ill, and that their "life-style" be recognized as a permissible alternative to more traditional arrangements.

It was then that the "gay rights" parades began and homosexuals began to proclaim publicly their pride in deviant behavior. They organized clubs, not only in the large cities but also on college campuses and later in high schools. Publications like *Blueboy* and the *Advocate* found their way into respectable bookstores. Then, a little later, homosexual bookstores and publishing companies began to crank up. Everybody was suddenly out of the closet, homosexual was "in", and a small but substantial homosexual industry began to flourish.

---

[3] Ibid., 3–4.

American "liberals" were at first reluctant to equate the problems of homosexuals with those of women and Blacks. Many thought that the two were entirely separate issues, that Blacks and women were discriminated against because of what they were, and homosexuals were discriminated against because of what they had somehow become, a product of their environment after birth. Such "liberals", ardent in support of the civil rights movement and the women's movement, were distressed at the idea of "gay bashing" and were even able to consider endorsing legislation to prohibit the firing of homosexuals because of their sexual habits. But they still believed in traditional moral values and were convinced that homosexuality should be cured rather than canonized.

Among these "liberals" and "moderates" were some of the most influential people in the nation: editors and staff members of such major newspapers as the *New York Times,* the *Washington Post*, and the *Los Angeles Times;* reporters and producers of news programs on the major networks; columnists and contributors; and the leading academic minds of the Left. Some of these people were supportive of so-called gay rights, but many held back.

The leaders of the homosexual movement knew they would have to bring most of the doubters into the fold before they could achieve the kind of results that Blacks and feminists had enjoyed, so they laid out a strategy designed to move the entire left and left-center into their camp. This strategy was multi-pronged and included the following major thrusts.

A. THE TRANSFORMATION OF THE RHETORIC

One of the first things the homosexuals had to do was to change the language used to talk about their issues. They realized that the "diction", or "vocabulary", in use up until the 1960s carried with it the associations of past attitudes. Then, too, there were as yet no words to describe some of the concepts they wanted to promote in their attack on traditional morality. So they simply replaced old words with new ones and made up terms to denote ideas or things that no one else yet believed in.

1. *"Gay"*

Such words as *queer*, *fairy*, and *faggot* were understandably objectionable to the homosexuals, since they carried with them heavily hostile connotations. But what was wrong with *homosexual*, a term that to most people was purely denotative? *Homosexual* was a word that the homosexuals themselves had used comfortably for generations and that the medical profession recognized as neutral and therefore "scientific". When heterosexuals wanted to find a term that was acceptable in all quarters, they too said "homosexual".

And that, of course, was part of the problem. In the first place, homosexuals wanted to name themselves. They did not want to accept a designation that was part of the common vocabulary, something produced by a consensus of the enemy. They were on the threshold of a new existence, and they wanted new language to define that existence. Adam had named all the creatures in Eden. In the America of the late twentieth century, the homosexual was the New Adam.

But even more important was the opportunity to replace a *neutral* term with a *positive* term, one that would not only denote what they were but also carry with it highly pleasant and seductive connotations. Once such a word was in place, they could use it to attract people to their cause.

So they chose the term *gay*, which had been used in France to describe homosexuals. There *gai* or *gaie* had connotations slightly different from its English counterpart, since it suggested "carelessness" and hence a certain moral laxity. But in English *gay* meant "happy and carefree", a state of mind that most people achieve only occasionally and that lasts only a brief period of time.

So when men or women stopped being "homosexual" and started being "gay", the effect on the public imagination was subtle but palpable. Such people were no longer merely defined by their sexual habits but were also presented as having a certain lighthearted happiness about them that others by implication lacked. In this connotative sense, then, "gay was good".

This connotation also implicitly countered an argument, made by all of the psychotherapists quoted in Chapter One, that homosexuality was the product of an unhappy and abnormal childhood and therefore a troubled and troubling aberration. Such an attitude, considered enlightened even in the late 1960s and early 1970s, was precisely what the homosexuals wanted to discourage in the recalcitrant liberals, and the word *gay* began to undermine that concept, if ever so slightly.

Thus the new word that homosexuals used for themselves was a small, shrewd argument in behalf of their cause rather than merely a synonym for "homosexual", but its widespread adoption was slow in coming. In 1969, for example, the *Village Voice*, then the most influential newspaper among homosexuals, refused to use the word and was attacked by the Gay Liberation Front, which demanded that the new rhetoric be adopted.[4] But it wasn't until 1987 that the *New York Times* finally capitulated and authorized the word *gay* without quotation marks. When they did so, the *Advocate* took special note of the shift in policy, realizing the philosophical movement that it implied.

> The word *gay* is acceptable, the *New York Times* has finally decided.
>
> After years of refusing to use *gay* except in the name of an organization or in quoted material, the newspaper's writers are now allowed to use the word as an adjective.
>
> The change was praised by gay activists in New York, who in meetings and letters have long urged the *Times* to alter its policy.

4 Ibid., 6.

Many reporters and editors at the *Times* had also chafed under the style rule banning *gay*. Following the change, one editorial employee commented, "Everyone sort of thinks it was a long time in coming. We have *Ms.* [also recently allowed] and now we have *gay*, so we're inching into the 20th century."[5]

Once the word *gay* became a part of the official homosexual lexicon, however, the gurus of the movement began to argue over its true significance. What was the difference between being "gay" and being merely "homosexual"?

One explanation is that of David Fernbach, who says that "homosexuals" are merely people who prefer sex partners of the same sex but that "gayness" is a matter of gender: "Gay men, in other words, really are effeminate."[6]

But most discussion tends to make "gayness" something much more than mere effeminacy, suggesting that it is a different way of looking at the entire world—and a superior one. Indeed, the very adoption of the term itself has unleashed a plenthora of words on the subject of cultural differences that define what it means to be "gay". Dennis Altman, perhaps the most perceptive and coherent interpreter of homosexuality, has said that the phrase *gay culture* has at least four different meanings:

> The first is that of life style, which is becoming as important as class and ethnicity in defining identities in America. The second is by way of those aesthetic products, usually literature or representational art (realistic paintings, sculpture, and photographs) that clearly grow out of this gay life style. . . .
>
> Much more difficult to define are the two other ways in which the term "gay culture" is used. The first is the assumption that all art produced by "gay people" is part of "gay culture". . . . The second idea is more complex. At its simplest it argues that the homosexual sensibility is a product of being a minority.[7]

This esoteric and at times pretentious analysis has grown out of the adoption of the word *gay* and goes on continually

[5] *Advocate* (July 21, 1987), 14.
[6] David Fernbach, in Altman, 56.
[7] Altman, 147–48.

among homosexuals, providing them with endless hours of entertainment and a "literature" to study in the growing number of "gay and lesbian studies" programs in colleges and universities. So the introduction of this new word *gay* into the political vocabulary of the nation has been tremendously successful, one of the great victories of the "gay rights movement".

2. *"Homophobe" and "Homophobic"*

After creating their own word for themselves and imposing it on a reluctant majority, the homosexuals then cast around for a word to designate their enemies — that is, the "straight" community, and more particularly, those who opposed the toleration of homosexual practices. The word *straight*, in vogue during the 1960s, wasn't pejorative enough. It didn't make a statement about what was wrong with these people, at least in the eyes of militant "gays". Therefore, it wasn't a weapon in the struggle for "freedom and power".

So the homosexuals came up with the term *homophobe*, which is now a term of abuse to be hurled at their enemies. When analyzed, of course, the word is almost nonsensical. Literally it seems to mean "fear of sameness": "homo" meaning "same" + "phobe" meaning "fear". But of course it is supposed to mean "fear of homosexuals", and hence fear of those who are "different" from oneself. (I suppose there are those who will argue that "fear of homosexuals" and "fear of sameness" stem from identical roots, but it is too tortuous an argument to follow.)

The use of the terms *homophobe* and *homophobia* affirms that those who oppose the so-called normalization of homosexual behavior are motivated by *fear* rather than by moral or religious principles. It also moves the discourse further away from the scholarly opinion that homosexuals are disturbed people by saying that it is those who disapprove of them who are mentally unbalanced, that *they* are in the grips of a "phobia" — clearly an abnormal condition.

"Phobia" also tends to dignify the homosexual by suggesting that he or she is formidable enough to excite terror rather
than mere loathing or discomfort. Great and powerful enemies fill us with fear; lesser enemies merely make us queasy or
uncomfortable. Most people who have been called
"homophobes" would probably laughingly deny that their
feelings were so strong or so cowardly; but at this point it
really doesn't matter, since the homosexuals have made it an
acceptable term in political discourse. That means that, know-
ingly or unknowingly, people who accept the validity of the
term have also accepted its underlying assumptions.

It is difficult to say whether the term *gay* or the term
homophobe has done more to alter public perception of the conflict between the advocates of sexual deviance and sexual nor-
malcy. However, one thing is certain: the use of the two in
tandem has had a profound effect on the dialogue concerning
these crucial issues and has tipped the scales, perhaps irrevers-
ibly, in favor of the homosexuals.

3. "Sexual Orientation", Formerly "Sexual Preference"

For a long while the homosexuals used the phrase *sexual preference* as an alternative to *sexual perversion* or *sexual deviation*,
two medical descriptions that had very bad connotations for
the community at large. A perversion, after all, was an undesirable distortion of something natural, and a deviation
implied the existence of heterosexuality as a recognized norm.
Thus, if homosexual behavior was perversion or deviation,
then it was not far from being "queer", and above all homosexuals wanted to be regarded as somehow "natural" and
"normal".

So at first they talked about sexual conduct as no more than
a "preference". You prefer vanilla; I prefer chocolate. You prefer baseball; I prefer football. You prefer bed partners of the
opposite sex; I prefer bed partners of the same sex.

At first this phrase seemed to work well for the homosexuals, particularly in conjunction with the idea of homosexuality as "an alternate life-style". Both "sexual preference" and "alternate life-style" trivialized sex by reducing it to nothing more than a quirk of personal preference.

But soon the phrase *sexual preference* began to get in the way of the agenda. One of the arguments that had proven most successful in the political arena was the idea that homosexuality was inherited, that it was the result of genetic or hormonal factors that were beyond the control of the individual, that homosexuals had sex with one another because they had to. Thus it was something "natural" and "normal" *for them*.

As noted in Chapter One, this argument was made by using a few isolated studies and by ignoring a substantial body of medical and psychological opinion; but the homosexuals discovered that the press—always sentimentalists where liberal causes were concerned—had made little or no effort to check the validity of the "argument from heredity". Soon they were all saying that homosexuals were "born that way" and that it was therefore unjust to deny them anything they wanted.

Such an acceptance of this highly tenuous argument delighted the homosexual activists, but it did dictate one rhetorical shift: sexuality could no longer be a "preference", since "preference" implied "choice", and the new line of argument was narrowly deterministic.

So they came up with "sexual orientation", and though some journalists still haven't gotten the message, more often than not homosexuality is now referred to in the press as an "orientation" rather than a "perversion", "deviation", or even "preference".

4. *"Alternate Life-Style"*

Again, here is a phrase that has a number of assumptions built into its meaning. It was invented (or appropriated) to counter the idea that homosexual behavior was immoral conduct.

Instead (the phrase argues), such activities are nothing more than "style", like living in the country or wearing blue jeans or traveling all the time. "Style" may reflect taste or background or idiosyncracy, but it doesn't have anything to do with morality. You would not get away with saying that raping and killing young women was nothing more than Ted Bundy's "life-style".

As for the word *alternate*, it further softens the idea that a "life-style" may radically set someone apart from the rest of the community. If homosexuality is simply an *alternate* life-style, then it is somehow equal to opposing life-styles, just another valid option in a "pluralistic society".

In many ways this phrase does more than *gay* and *homophobe* to exonerate homosexuality from all charges previously made against it. As soon as you have admitted that such sexual devi-ation is an "alternate life-style", you have effectively ruled out the idea that it is either immoral or an illness to be treated and cured. Thus it is fair to say that anyone who uses the phrase has already conceded to the homosexuals everything they want in the argument to alter our society.

It is in recognition of this truth that so many people were disturbed when Surgeon General C. Everett Koop, a good surgeon but a careless and ill-trained student of language, said in his *Surgeon General's Report:* "Some Americans have diffi-culties in dealing with the subjects of sex, sexual practices, and alternate lifestyles."[8]

5. *"Discovering or Exploring One's Sexuality"*

This is another phrase used by the Surgeon General in his *Report*, when he says: "Adolescents and preadolescents are those whose behavior we wish to especially [sic] influence because of their vulnerability when they are exploring

[8] C. Everett Koop, *The Surgeon General's Report on Acquired Immune Defi-ciency Syndrome* (Washington, D.C.: 1986), 4.

their own sexuality (heterosexual and homosexual) and perhaps experimenting with drugs."[9]

The homosexuals are particularly fond of either version of this phrase because once again it "begs a question"—that is, assumes something that needs to be proven. In this case, the phrase implies that there is already a sexuality there that, like the New World, is fully created and waiting to be "discovered" and "explored".

Clearly, if such is the case, then by the time of adolescence, there are no more choices to be made, there is nothing to be created or developed. Sexuality has been predetermined, either by inherited factors or by abnormal conditions in childhood. But either way the phrase plays into the hands of those who want to argue that individuals can do little about "sexual orientation" once they have reached adolescence. As we have seen in Chapter Three, several excellent programs seem to be disproving that thesis.

6. "Family Partner"

In recent homosexual literature the phrase *family partner* has begun to appear. While it has not yet gained the currency of these other examples, it bids fair to emerge as a very important rhetorical weapon in the fight for insurance and tax breaks and, more importantly, the right to adopt children.

Again, you can understand the full meaning of the phrase only when you realize what it is intended to counteract. One of the chief arguments against the "normalizing" of homosexuality is the degree to which such a policy would undercut the supremacy of the traditional family as the foundation of American life.

A "traditional family", after all, is a man and woman who are married to one another and who may or may not have children (though children are usually implied). Needless to say,

[9] Ibid.

the idea that such a unit is to be given special consideration in American society infuriates the homosexuals, since thus far they have been outside this circle by definition.

Indeed, homosexuals have been perceived as the "antifamily", the ultimate enemy of society's basic unit, since they hope to see a significant percentage of young people leave the idea of family behind and join their ranks, where there is no thought of procreation with sex, only immediate pleasure. Traditionally mothers and fathers, believing in the family as the fundamental social good, have guarded their children against the homosexual child molester, believing that early homosexual experience will warp a youngster and send him off in the wrong direction, away from the proper family experience.

Homosexuals have long proclaimed that early homosexual experiences don't predetermine "sexual orientation", but they have not gotten far with this argument—since parents instinctively believe that such experiences may indeed pervert the child. So the idea of the family has remained an irksome and at times insurmountable barrier between homosexuals and the achievement of their ultimate goals.

Recently homosexuals have adopted a new tactic, particularly in dealing with the traditional judicial prejudice in favor of families. They have started to talk about their own "families"—hence the phrase "family partners" to describe two men or two women living together and having deviant sexual relations. In using such a phrase, the homosexuals are saying: "See, we have families too; and they are not substantially different from other families, except that we are having sex in a slightly different way from married couples." They are also adding, by implication: "And since two homosexuals living together constitute 'family partners', we should be allowed all the perquisites of married heterosexual partners, including tax exemptions and other legal advantages, as well as the right to adopt and rear children on an equal basis."

This latter-day insistence that they too have "families" is an acknowledgment on the part of the homosexual activists that they have been most vulnerable when faced by opponents who appeal to the American commitment to family life as a positive and unquestioned good. In fact, many of the organizations opposing them have the word *family* in their names (Focus on the Family, the American Family Association, United Families of America, the Family Research Council), and others have programs and publications with *family* in the titles.

It now remains to be seen whether the media will pick up this new phrase used by homosexuals and repeat it often enough that it becomes an integral part of the dialogue, thereby further confusing the American public, which generally makes the right decision on such matters when it is not subverted by false rhetoric or erroneous data.

This reinvention of the language has been a chief weapon in the homosexual arsenal, one that can be used on every battle-front: in the political arena, in the courts, in the academy, in the churches, and in the marketplace. No one has used language to greater advantage than homosexuals have, in part because in the American press they have a sympathetic and at times unthinking ally. Without the dogged cooperation of mainline newspapers and the television networks, it might have been easier to talk about these crucial issues with a clear and impartial language. Now we must either reinvent the vocabulary, a stratagem that the homosexuals and the press would fight every inch of the way, or we must somehow make our arguments heard while at the same time bearing the burden of all these loaded words and phrases.

This, of course, is precisely what the homosexual language manipulators had in mind.

B. THE REDEFINITION OF HOMOSEXUALITY

Most Americans over forty remember a time when homosexuality was little talked about, in part because it was an unpleasant subject, in part because people didn't want to make homosexuals feel any worse than they felt already. For it was the consensus—never challenged until very recently—that at best these sad creatures were products of a disturbed childhood and at worst slaves to unnatural appetites that they had encouraged in themselves. Unless they become public spectacles or molested children, they were left alone.

"Queer bashing" was something you heard tales about but seldom if ever witnessed. Homosexual bars flourished in large cities, and occasionally there were ugly incidents involving the police. However, for the most part everyone preferred to ignore the widespread and routine violations of the law rather than to expose such goings-on to public scrutiny. "Live and let live" was the policy of most American cities in dealing with homosexuals and what they did.

But the "gay rights movement" changed all that. Those who devised its grand strategy saw an opportunity in the late 1960s to revise the rules and to do so in their favor. In the wake of the women's movement, with its bitter accusations and its brooding analysis of the feminine mystique, homosexuals began to assert their own historical martyrdom and to reconstruct a history of oppression to rival that of Blacks and women.

Instead of remaining in the shadow land of their own world, homosexuals came out in the open, admitting their sexual differences and publicly proclaiming a pride in their behavior. They were, they argued, the ultimate victims of Western history, persecuted by a "homophobic" Church, punished and manipulated in such a way that they had for generations been ashamed of themselves. Now, in the second half of the twentieth century, they were ready to affirm their true identity and to claim their rightful place in American society.

It had worked for Blacks. It had worked for women. It would also work for homosexuals.

But of course there was an obvious difference between Blacks and women on the one hand and homosexuals on the other. The first two had been discriminated against because of what they *were*. Homosexuals were discriminated against because of what they *did*. Blacks and women were born that way. Homosexuals were somehow or other "made". No one had ever argued that just being Black or female was immoral. Homosexual behavior had been regarded as immoral since at least the time of Moses.

These seemingly insurmountable differences posed a challenge for the homosexual leadership. However, with the spirit of the times on their side (America was feeling guilty about itself) and with the press willing to give credence to anyone who said the nation was wicked, they went about the task of redefining just who and what they were.

The homosexuals' first task was to alter the perception of homosexual behavior as something learned and possibly taken up by choice. The oldest and most widely held view until midcentury was probably the "moral explanation"—the conviction that people became homosexuals because somewhere along the way they made a conscious choice to try deviant behavior as an alternative to normal intercourse. This explanation was based on biblical denunciations of homosexual behavior (see Chapter Three) and the "old-fashioned" assumption that to some degree the human will was free.

By midcentury, however, Freudian psychology had finally made its mark on popular thought. More and more people were beginning to believe that homosexuals were the product of an irregular and disturbed childhood, that the possessive and overly protective mother in combination with the weak or abusive father produced the homosexual boy, while the lesbian was produced by similar familial discordance. How many Americans had come to explain homosexuality totally in these terms is anyone's guess, but educated people were more and more inclined to give some credence to these influences.

Needless to say, neither of these explanations was completely satisfactory to the militant homosexual. The first impugned his character, and the second turned him into a bundle of helpless responses to external stimuli. Neither justified his conduct in a way that made him a martyr to society's irrational bigotry. The second explanation was a little more satisfying than the first, but it still left homosexuality as something unnatural and monstrous.

What was needed was a third explanation, one that would put homosexuals into the same category of innocent sufferers as the Blacks, who were indeed the victims of tragic and unjust historical circumstances. Blacks were clearly the paradigm for homosexuals to contemplate. First, they were born black, a genetic trait beyond their control. Second, they found themselves in a predominantly white world, a world where race was an all-important determinant of social and economic advancement and therefore sometimes produced a particularly cruel kind of persecution. If only homosexuals could make the argument that their condition was in some way genetic and that they had been unjustly persecuted by a self-centered and overbearing majority culture.

It is difficult to say whether the demand for such evidence produced a sudden supply, or whether homosexuals began to develop this argument after discovering that a few researchers were indeed convinced that heredity did play a role in the development of homosexuality. As suggested in Chapter One, social scientists are often like politicians—too often they find what they are looking for in the statistics available.

One thing is certain: by the late 1960s there were a few tentative endocrinological and hormonal studies that seemed to suggest biological determinism, enough for homosexuals to declare themselves blameless products of nature and to begin mounting an attack on the same mean-spirited and unjust society that had produced the Vietnam War.

But there was one obstacle to their stratagem: the American Psychiatric Association still said that homosexuality was an abnormal condition, a mental disorder in need of treatment. This determination was contained in the *Diagnostic and Statistical Manual of Psychiatric Disorders*, the bible of psychopathology. Because the American Psychiatric Association controlled what went into that book, they ultimately held the fate of the homosexual movement in their hands.

So the homosexuals were really left with no choice: they would have to take over the American Psychiatric Association. Otherwise their political arguments would be easily refuted by reference to the *Diagnostic and Statistical Manual*.

At first this may have seemed like an impossible task, something that could be accomplished only in a two-part miniseries. But on closer investigation, it really wasn't as difficult as it appeared. In the first place, while a significant portion of psychiatrists belonged to the American Psychiatric Association, only a small percentage actually attended national meetings, and even fewer were actively involved in the politics of the organization. Thus, a concerted effort to storm the organization and take it over was by no means a futile dream. Indeed, that is precisely what the homosexuals did.

I have dealt with this outrageous campaign in Chapter One. Suffice it to say that *Homosexuality and American Psychiatry* by Ronald Bayer has probably served as a blueprint for homosexual activism in the 1980s, a how-to-do-it book for those who want to run roughshod over organized society.

Bayer tells more than he intended in this remarkable story of intrigue, moral bullying, physical intimidation, and downright dishonesty. It would be impossible for a disinterested person to read this book without completely discounting the actions that the American Psychiatric Association took in its 1973 meeting, when a homosexual horde came riding down on them like Genghis Khan's army, screaming, waving their arms, with orders to take no prisoners.

Once the homosexuals had captured the American Psychiatric Association and subsequently the American Psychological Association, they had leverage on the organizational structure of the counseling profession. At that point, they began to feed the popular media information concerning the few studies that seemed to support the genetic or hormonal origins of deviant behavior. Anyone scanning the *New York*

Times over the past ten years for information on this subject would be struck by the number of articles that repeat these same findings over and over again, without any reference to the many other studies that seem to refute or mitigate such a view. It is interesting to note as well that it has been easier to find a dissenting view among homosexuals than among the staid leftist publications that picked up the homosexual line and repeated it until it became part of the canon of liberalism, its newest and most cherished prejudice.

Within a period of less than a decade the homosexuals were able to control the "data" of the debate. That is, they were able to dictate those scientific "facts" that must be accepted without question if one is to be allowed to speak authoritatively on this question. The "facts" were simple: (1) homosexuality was pre-determined before birth; (2) homosexuals had no choice over what they were or how they behaved; and (3) environmental factors, including the presence and attentions of homosexuals, could not affect a child adversely and *cause* homosexuality.

The conclusions derived from these "facts" were inevitable: (1) like Blacks, homosexuals were victims of ignorance and prejudice; (2) they needed protection from the persecution of the majority; and (3) laws had to be passed with this objective.

C. FOCUSING ON WHAT HOMOSEXUALS ARE RATHER THAN WHAT THEY DO

As homosexuals were developing a pseudoscientific case for "gay rights", they were also diverting attention from the one aspect of their cause that was most vulnerable: their sexual habits. Most people simply found the idea of homoerotic behavior disgusting—when they thought about it at all (and heterosexuals usually preferred to think about something else). The truth was, they really knew very little of what went on in the homosexual world.

But the homosexuals were well aware of how ignorant the general public was concerning their practices, and their campaign to establish the predetermined nature of their "sexual orientation" continued to occupy the center of the public arena. As Dennis Altman put it:

> The greatest single victory of the gay movement over the past decade has been to shift the debate from behavior to identity, thus forcing opponents into a position where they can be seen as attacking the civil rights of homosexual citizens rather than attacking specific and (as they see it) antisocial behavior.[10]

Once you read this statement by a leading interpreter of the "gay rights movement", you realize how crucial the takeover of the two professional associations was to the success of the homosexual agenda. The putsch established the homosexual as a victim and as a consequence made him a recognizable stereotype to the liberal establishment, a necessary prelude to any kind of political activism. Liberalism—which is really a reactionary force in our society—has long since passed the time when it can entertain new ideas or even modify old ones. Liberals can act only when they can see the problems confronting them in terms of old, familiar stereotypes.

In the 1930s, during the first presidential term of Franklin Delano Roosevelt, it was conservatives who thought in stereotypes and therefore resisted any change in the status quo. Today the liberals believe that it is still 1936, they have just won a landslide victory over Alf Landon, and they can't wait for January, when they will raise taxes and inaugurate a host of new government programs. This time the programs will be for homosexuals, since they are the minority victims of the 1980s. As Altman has suggested, the accomplishment of this transformation within the short span of two decades is one of the most remarkable political achievements of an extraordinary age.

[10] Altman, 9.

D. THE ORGANIZATION OF PUBLIC DEMONSTRATIONS

Much of the success of homosexual activists lies in their ability to organize demonstrations, orchestrate spectacular happenings, and disrupt the public meetings and deliberations of their opponents. Martin Luther King, Jr., at the height of his influence, was able to bring together much larger crowds than the homosexuals. But not since King's day has anyone matched what the "gay liberation" movement has achieved over the past few years.

For example, on October 11, 1987, between 100,000 and 150,000 homosexuals gathered in Washington, D.C., paraded down Pennsylvania Avenue, and then convened for speeches, songs, and "marriage" ceremonies on the steps of the U.S. Supreme Court building. Later, in their own press accounts they reported attendance of 500,000 to 600,000—the usual inflation of estimates by local authorities, but even the truth was impressive. And there is reason to believe that the numbers may be larger in the future.

For one thing, homosexuals have money to spend on such activities, and, without children to take care of, they are much freer and more mobile than normal people. Then, too, they are by definition a politically activated community, one that from the outset has considered itself under siege and is therefore forever planning defenses and counterattacks.

As a number of analysts have pointed out, the homosexuals define themselves as much by their aggressive political behavior as by what they do sexually. Thus, while political activism is unusual behavior for most people—something the average family has no time or inclination to pursue—the uncloseted homosexual is compulsively political, since it is just another way of announcing his "sexual orientation" to the world.

What more public baring of his soul than to march down Fifth Avenue in the Gay Pride Parade, come to Washington and dramatize his "sexual orientation" to the nation as a whole, or to come to a meeting of "straights" and disrupt the

proceedings in the service of "gay rights"? Thus have homosexuals affirmed on a communal level what they have affirmed
in their private lives—a commitment to homosexuality as a
way of looking at and responding to the world.

Two of the homosexuals' important political organizations
are the following.

1. *The National Gay and Lesbian Task Force*

The National Gay Task Force, later called the National Gay
and Lesbian Task Force, was founded in 1973 as a political lobbying group. Though it has never numbered more than a few
thousand members, it has nonetheless been enormously
influential. Enrique T. Rueda, in *The Homosexual Network*,
describes its successes as follows:

> It was due to the efforts of the NGTF that the American Psy-
> chiatric Association officially took homosexuality from its list
> of mental illnesses. The NGTF was also instrumental in making
> the White House accessible and willing to lend a favorable ear to
> the leadership of the homosexual movement during the Carter
> Administration. This and the introduction of several prohomo-
> sexual statutes in the U.S. Congress—to a great extent also the
> work of the NGTF—exemplify the high degree of acceptance of
> homosexuality by the U.S. government. . . . The NGTF has
> been influential in causing a number of U.S. agencies (e.g.,
> Internal Revenue Service, Bureau of Prisons, Federal Commu-
> nications Commission) to make regulatory decisions which
> favor the acceptance of homosexuality as a legitimate lifestyle.
> Another area in which the NGTF has been active is the promo-
> tion of the homosexual ideology in corporations by the adop-
> tion of "homosexual rights" policies.[11]

In the early days the organization was dominated by its lesbian codirector, Jean O'Leary, a former nun, who was
appointed to commissions by both President Jimmy Carter
and Mayor Ed Koch of New York. She was succeeded as codi-

---

[11] Enrique T. Rueda, *The Homosexual Network* (Old Greenwich, Conn.:
1982), 157.

rector by Lucia Valeska, who also overshadowed her male counterpart, Charles F. Bryden.

Recently, however, the structure has undergone changes. Currently Executive Director Jeffrey Levi is the most visible member of the organization, which has achieved a respectability no one could have predicted fifteen years ago.

Essentially, the NGLTF is the homosexual counterpart of the Americans for Democratic Action, an organization liberal in its politics but operating within the pale of the current political system. More and more Executive Director Jeff Levi has become the spokesman for the "gay rights movement", the person to whom the liberal press turns for the homosexual perspective on current events.

While Levi is considered radical by many "straights", he is by no means a fringe figure in the homosexual movement. Indeed, some radicals have criticized the group from the beginning as entirely too establishmentarian.

Arthur Evans, a more militant figure, said this about the NGLTF when it was still known as the National Gay Task Force:

> A more subtle emphasis on professionalism and middle class values is found in the National Gay Task Force, the nation's leading gay liberal political group. NGTF greatly admires the ideal of the highly educated, middle class, professional gay person. It emphasizes the importance of a "professional approach" to gay liberation. NGTF runs itself internally on the model of a professional business organization. Interestingly, the phrase "Task Force" is a military-bureaucrat term, first used by the U.S. Navy to denote a particular group of differing specialists under the leadership of one commander. [12]

(Incidentally, the addition of the word *lesbian* to the title of this organization indicates some of the problems that continue to arise between male and female homosexuals in the movement. Some lesbians have come to believe that the word *gay*— since it has been most frequently applied to men—does not

[12] Arthur Evans, quoted in Altman, 126.

really suit their differing sexuality and, for that matter, life in general. Thus the word *lesbian* was added to the name as a means of gaining their wholehearted support.)

The NGLTF membership is currently estimated at approximately 10,000 members, an increase of about 5,000 over the previous year. At its meeting in November of 1987 the organization's board approved a budget of $1.5 million, an amount twice the previous year's figure. This increase was predicated on the assumption that the organization could triple the number of new members, increase by nearly three times the amount they had previously solicited by telephone, and earn four times the income earned last year from special events. Among the new programs on the drawing board as the result of this expansion program are a "lesbian and gay families project" to fight for adoption and custody rights for homosexual parents and would-be parents and a "minority project" to address the needs and problems of ethnic homosexuals.

Perhaps the most important item on the NGLTF's agenda in 1988 was the political campaign, which the organization hoped to influence, at both the state and federal levels. Indeed, they had already made an impact on one of the major political parties.

In a fund-raising appeal, sent out early in February, Jeff Levi announced that the NGLTF had sent out questionnaires to all of the declared nominees for President in both the Democratic and Republican parties. The question asked was the following: "As President, would you sign the gay/lesbian civil rights bill now pending in Congress that would prohibit discrimination based on sexual orientation?"

Levi reported the following results: *"For the first time in American political history—every Democratic candidate for the presidency has pledged to sign that bill into law"*[13] (emphasis in the original).

---

[13] Jeff Levi, in "ACTION ALERT" letter, Feb. 5, 1988.

It was indeed a historic victory for this pressure group. Ten years ago no serious presidential candidate would have considered such a commitment, and even four years ago Walter Mondale did not go so far. Levi was quick to press his advantage:

> I wanted to share this news with you as quickly as possible, because it was your continued support that has made our Presidential Campaign Effort possible.
>
> Now, for the first time ever, we have on the record the views of each Democratic candidate on lesbian and gay rights, as well as dozens of other crucial issues such as AIDS treatment, prevention and patient care.
>
> But now that we know where the Democratic candidates stand, our work is just beginning. For example:
> *None* of the Republican candidates has yet agreed to support civil rights protection for lesbians and gays.
>
> In fact, only one Republican candidate even bothered to return our survey in time for the results to be announced publicly. Their *silence* can only be viewed as approval of the Reagan Administration's policy of discrimination and disregard.[14]

The letter did not mention that the lone Republican who answered the NGLTF questionnaire was George Bush, who wrote: "No group should have special privileges granted by government."[15] Levi came back later in the month with a follow-up solicitation in which he promised these election-year activities:

> Task Force staff will be active at both the Republican and Democratic conventions. We will be a visible presence—not as advocates for a particular party or candidate—but as spokespersons for our community.
>
> The Task Force will work with local gay and lesbian community organizations to register and educate voters.
>
> We will provide technical assistance to local groups so that they can construct and administer questionnaires to candidates for Congress.

---

[14] Ibid.
[15] George Bush, quoted in *Advocate* (Mar. 1, 1988), 14.

We will document the positions of all newly elected Senators and Representatives so that we can hold them accountable after the election.[16]

Though the National Gay and Lesbian Task Force does not endorse candidates or identify with a specific party, it is a "political lobbying organization" and therefore does not qualify for a tax-deductible status—a fact that may explain to some degree its modest growth over the past few years. In debt over $100,000 just three years ago, it is now reaping the rewards of homosexual gains over the past twenty-four months and the visibility gained by the movement in its 1987 Washington march.

But the fact is: the National Gay and Lesbian Task Force is not an enormous organization, certainly not in comparison with conservative groups like the American Family Association, Eagle Forum, and Moral Majority. Each of these boasts a membership in six figures.

Indeed, it is sometimes difficult to believe that the homosexual movement is as formidable as it seems, given the fact that the NGLTF fluctuates wildly in membership, with 10,000 reported by Rueda in 1982, only 5,000 in 1986, and then 10,000 again in 1987.

But you can't quarrel with success. Regardless of the relatively small size of the NGLTF, it has taken on the most well organized and powerful adversaries, including the federal government itself, and come out the winner. If tenacity, shrewdness, courage, and dedication were the only qualities used in judging such an organization, you would have to admire the magnificent scope of their achievement. They have operated on the national stage with an effectiveness that few, if any, lobbying groups have surpassed over the past fifteen years.

---

[16] Levi, in letter addressed "Dear NGLTF Member", Feb. 26, 1988.

2. *The Human Rights Campaign Fund*

The Human Rights Campaign Fund (HRCF) is a homosexual political action committee (PAC). Unlike the National Gay and Lesbian Task Force, it collects and distributes funds for the election of specific candidates to public office. In addition, since 1987 it has maintained at least three lobbyists in Washington to make certain that those candidates who have received support from HRCF are reminded of their obligations to vote for prohomosexual legislation of all kinds.

In 1986, when HRCF was ranked as the sixteenth-largest independent PAC in the nation, Vic Basile, the executive director, boasted that the group supported over a hundred candidates for the House and Senate. By 1988 the group was listed ninth and had raised over $1 million for an election-year war chest. Through fund-raising dinners in Boston, New York, and Washington—attended by such celebrities as Senator John Kerry and Mathilde Krim of the American Foundation for AIDS Research—HRCF continues to add to its financial resources. The *Gay Community News* of Boston reported that the organization raised $250,000 at one such occasion on the night prior to the 1987 march on Washington.

On September 27, 1987, the principal speaker at the annual New York dinner was Coretta Scott King, who criticized the U.S. Supreme Court for continuing to support state sodomy laws and warned against "the mounting assault on civil rights in this country".

"I am here tonight", she said,

> to express my solidarity with the gay and lesbian community in your struggle for civil and human rights in America and around the world. I believe all Americans who believe in freedom, tolerance and human rights have a responsibility to oppose bigotry and prejudice based on sexual orientation. . . . If sexual relations between consenting adults are not part of the right to privacy . . . then American democracy is in trouble.[17]

[17] Coretta Scott King, quoted in *Advocate* (Nov. 11, 1986), 17.

Lest anyone become too disturbed by the amount of money being raised and spent by this PAC, it is significant to note that when Senator Helms and I introduced bills in both houses of Congress to prohibit the federal government from funding educational materials that promoted homosexuality, the House version passed by a vote of 368 to 47 and the Senate version by 94 to 2.

Vic Basile acknowledges such defeats, but he explains them as follows:

> We've got to realize and accept that courage is not a common commodity on Capitol Hill. When the Right forces a vote on homosexuality, we're in trouble. When we keep focused on AIDS and civil rights, we do pretty well. . . . There is more courage behind the closed doors of the conference committee.[18]

With that statement in mind, it is interesting to note what HRCF's chief legislative priority was in 1987–88 and what became of it. As Basile himself put it in a fund-raising letter full of extravagant rhetoric and irresponsible charges:

> *Our top legislative priority* on Capitol Hill now is the creation of a comprehensive "Manhattan Project" on AIDS. Just as when America's leaders cleared all the bureaucratic hurdles and focused all of our brightest minds on building an atomic bomb with astonishing success and speed . . . we can once again mobilize our best scientific talent to fight the common enemy— AIDS—if the necessary government funding is made available!
>
> The National Academy of Sciences has recommended $1 billion for AIDS research and $1 billion for education . . . and we're still at less than half of that funding level today. It's time to do more. Much more.[19]

And they did! They focused on AIDS rather than on the narrower homosexual agenda, and the result was an appropriations bill far greater than anything the current AIDS crisis could justify, particularly in the field of education, where the

---

[18] Victor Basile, quoted in *Gay Community News* (Nov. 17, 1987).
[19] Basile, in an undated letter addressed "Dear Friend", 3.

amount approved was even larger than the $1 billion recom-
mended. As Basile boasted to his constituency:

> And we're the most experienced and best-suited PAC and lob-
> bying organization to lead such an ambitious and critical battle
> on Capitol Hill.
>   Simply put, each dollar you send us now will help us secure
> 100 or even 1,000 times as many dollars in new government
> funding.[20]

In addition to funding liberal supporters in Congress, the
Human Rights Campaign Fund also spends a great deal of
money on information campaigns and propaganda. In 1986,
for example, according to the *New York Native*, a homosexual
newspaper, HRCF spent $10,000 on legal expenses for those
arrested at the Third International Conference on AIDS in
Washington. It spent a great deal more than that on a full-page
ad denouncing Senator Jesse Helms that was carried in the *Boston Globe*, the *New York Times*, the *Washington Post*, the *Los
Angeles Times*, and several other newspapers throughout the
country.

These two organizations, the NGLTF and the HRCF—
relatively small in numbers though well financed—have managed to push homosexual legislation with striking success.
Even during the Reagan administration—ostensibly hostile to
their agenda—they managed to achieve signal victories, the
most recent of which was passage in the House of a bill
designed to set the stage for national "gay rights" legislation.

E. GETTING UNCLE SAM TO HELP

In January of 1989, The National Research Council came out
with a 589-page report *(AIDS: Sexual Behavior and Intravenous
Drug Use)*, which provided the homosexuals with a substantial

---

[20] Ibid.

weapon to use in their war against Christian churches. This report—funded by the U.S. Public Health Service to the tune of almost a half million dollars—said, among other things, that "some religions" stigmatized homosexual behavior and IV drug use, that such stigmatization constituted "social pathology", and that churches should "demand" of their adherents that they be sympathetic toward homosexual acts and the use of illegal drugs.

This report full of political opinions, unsupported generalizations, and polemical rhetoric was no more scientific than an issue of the *National Gay Rights Advocates Newsletter*. Fortunately, it received little attention in the national press; but it is clearly a source for homosexual activists to cite when they attempt to argue the scientific validity of their cause, particularly in their attacks on the Christian church—attacks which have grown shriller and more demanding over the past year.

In late June of 1989, the homosexual activists, working quietly behind the scenes, persuaded the U.S. Postal Service to grant them the right to cancel stamps for two days at a special Greenwich Village station, with a political slogan and a pictorial graphic showing two male symbols interlocked and two female symbols likewise interlocked.

Federal regulations specifically forbid messages that are "political" slogans or statements of "ideals". But with their usual facility, the homosexuals were able to get their cancellation mark approved by the Post Office without difficulty, and only after it had been announced did the public discover what new use the "gay" activists had made of the government. Despite written protests and angry phone calls that numbered in the thousands, the cancellations were allowed on the twenty-fourth and twenty-fifth of June—in memory of the twentieth anniversary of the "Stonewall incident", regarded as the beginning of the "gay rights movement". During all this, postal authorities continued to maintain that neither the slogan nor the event it was commemorating could be regarded as either "political" or the statement of an "ideal".

During this same period, the National Endowment for the Arts was also in difficulty with the American people over their support of homosexual activities. The Corcoran Museum announced that it was featuring a retrospective show by homosexual photographer Robert Mapplethorpe, who had died of AIDS. Mapplethorpe's show included photos of male sexual organs, nude and erotically posed tots, and two homosexuals engaged in sexual activity. It was obscene by almost anybody's standards except those of the community out of which it came—and a number of us in Congress made our revulsion known, as did several important grassroots organizations, most notably the American Family Association.

This time we were successful, and the Corcoran Museum cancelled the show. Well they might have. A number of members of Congress on both sides of the aisle were talking about cutting appropriations for the National Endowment for the Arts or else defunding the agency completely. I suspect as the result of this and other NEA-funded projects, there will be some revision of the way in which the Endowment is allowed to allocate its resources. No agency that uses tax dollars to support homosexual pornography should be given a free rein. It is typical of the times in which we live that the press should call the imposition of tougher guidelines "a stifling of free expression", as if artists had the inalienable right to be funded by the Federal government.

F. WHAT MUST BE DONE TO STOP THE HOMOSEXUAL MOVEMENT?

There is a sad and paradoxical twist to the political success of the homosexual movement. Within the past two years, AIDS has threatened to decimate the homosexual population. Indeed, many homosexuals have lamented the fact that just when they had gained an unprecedented freedom to live their lives as they wanted to, AIDS suddenly, mysteriously intervened and cut short their day in the sun.

Such an opinion, tragically ironic, is reminiscent of the man who complained that he was breaking his mule of the habit of eating, and just when he'd been on the brink of success, the mule died. It is precisely *because* of the "gay liberation movement" that AIDS has afflicted so many homosexual men. The very organizations presuming to speak for the welfare of homosexuals have insisted that the bathhouses remain open, that sex can still be "safe", that no one should be forced to take an HIV test, that no one can be warned when a sex partner is AIDS infected. If anyone suggests that the government take traditional health care measures to stop this disease from spreading, the National Gay and Lesbian Task Force, the Human Rights Campaign Fund, the Lambda Legal Defense, the National Gay Rights Advocates, and literally thousands of homosexual organizations nationwide rise up to block the way, shrieking their disapproval on grounds of "rights" unknown a decade ago. And what is worse, they have intimidated government officials at every level, as well as educators and reporters, forcing them to echo the expressions of outrage.

But of course, the end result of adopting such precautionary measures would be to save thousands and thousand of lives — mostly homosexual lives, since the homosexual population is primarily at risk from this terrible plague. Why, then, are the political activities of homosexual organizations principally directed at preventing government at every level from containing the spread of AIDS?

The answer to that question is complicated, and I'm not sure that anyone knows it for certain. However, some of the following factors are surely at work:

1. The homosexual leaders have been so preoccupied with the advancement of homosexual rights that they simply haven't been able to shift gears in order to save their constit-

uency from its own excesses. Let's face it, it is much easier to tell a group of people, "We're here to get you what you want", than it is to say, "This time the establishment is right; you must submit to the rules of civil authority or else die." Until AIDS, all the homosexuals wanted was to widen the sexual revolution; now, when they are its primary victims, their leadership still fights for the right to get AIDS and to infect others.

2. To admit the full ramifications of the appearance of AIDS, the homosexual leadership would be forced to acknowledge their own role in promoting the disease. As Randy Shilts has made clear in his book *And the Band Played On*, AIDS might never have reached epidemic proportions had not the homosexual bathhouses in New York and San Francisco been allowed to operate without significant opposition from law-enforcement agencies. After the disease was already rampant, Mayor Feinstein of San Francisco attempted to close down these HIV hives, but because of homosexual opposition, the court ruled that the bathhouses could be forced to follow "safe sex" practices but not forbidden to operate. And, indeed, the Lambda Defense and Education Fund, the National Gay Rights Advocates, and the ACLU have made it impossible to control promiscuity or to determine precisely who is and isn't infected with AIDS. Any reversal of position on such issues would be an admission of complicity in the deaths of thousands.

3. There is among the homosexual leadership as well as the rank and file a death wish that lies at the heart of all their pronouncements and actions. Everything they have done since the beginning of this disease has contributed to its spread—from the promotion of condoms in the face of known failure rates to the refusal to be tested or to allow the sexual contacts of AIDS-infected people to be told of their danger. Note in Chapter Three the advice of the Reverend Troy Perry to his friends not to be tested. Note the insistence of the NGRA that foreign AIDS victims continue to be admitted to this country. Note the statement of Lambda Legal Defense Fund's Tom

Stoddard that "AIDS requires a deliberate act of willfulness, a personal determination to put oneself in jeopardy." The whole AIDS epidemic may, in fact, be the acting out of a corporate death wish as widespread and compulsive as that of the lemmings.

So how do we address the kind of willful self-destruction that we are witnessing today? What can we do to help these poor people before they completely annihilate one another? In the next chapter I include some of the suggestions I have been offering for the past several years, and some new ones as well.

CHAPTER FIVE

The New Sex Education: Homosexuality

Thirty years ago some public schools taught students about sex, and some did not. No one can say for sure how many fell into the former category, but my guess would be a small percentage of the total. This lack of commitment to sex education on the part of most Americans was probably the result of a long-standing assumption that such matters were better discussed in the home and that classroom time was better spent in learning math, English, history, and languages.

The fact that parents often neglected to have that little talk with their children did not seem terribly important, since by junior high school virtually every youngster had gotten the word through an ancient and fairly active grapevine. I'll admit a lot of misinformation was passed around, some of it disturbing, most of it harmless. However, by and large no one was getting into a great deal of trouble.

For example, teenage pregnancy was not a nationwide problem, nor was illegitimate birth. These things happened only occasionally; when a girl got pregnant, the young man usually married her. To be sure, some of these marriages did not work out, but a surprising number did; and weighing all the pros and cons of sexual mores thirty years ago, I think most thoughtful Americans would say we were better off then than now.

Last year over 1 million unmarried teenagers got pregnant. Over 500,000 had their babies out of wedlock, and another 400,000 had abortions. These statistics don't begin to define the cost in human suffering, not only to the young women themselves but also to their families, to the young men with whom they were involved, and to the children produced by such liaisons. It is easy enough to say, as some people do, that abortion is a simple solution, both safe and pain free. However, the physical and mental trauma is often severe, even if the people involved are not sensitive to the moral issues involved in killing an unborn child.

Of course, organizations like Planned Parenthood and the Sex Information and Education Council of the United States (SIECUS) use the statistics cited above to argue in favor of sex education for all young Americans, maintaining that with more instruction in the use of birth control methods, none of these things would occur. Yet even as the amount of sex instruction has risen over the years, so has the pregnancy rate—not just the number of pregnancies, mind you, but the *rate* at which unmarried girls are becoming pregnant. In fact, there is an eerie correlation between the amount of money spent from state to state on sex education and the rise of pregnancies. Those states that spend very little money on such education have a low pregnancy rate. Those that spend a lot of money have a proportionally bigger problem. While these figures don't necessarily prove that sex education courses cause higher pregnancy rates, we can certainly say with confidence that such programs are not making a dent in the problem. Yet Planned Parenthood and SIECUS continue to push for more and more education about pills and condoms and IUDs, forever promising that in just a few more years we will turn the corner and begin to eliminate the problem.

In recent years another group has added its voice to the growing cry for more extensive and "explicit" sex education in our schools. That group is the organized homosexual movement.

The motives of Planned Parenthood and SIECUS are sometimes difficult to fathom. They seem to display an almost religious zeal for teaching young people how to become "sexually active", regardless of the consequences of their programs. But the motives of the homosexual movement are a little easier to read.

Clearly they see "explicit" and "nonjudgmental" sex education as a means of introducing young people to the practices of homosexuals. To "avoid bigotry" the public schools are being enjoined to teach heterosexuality and homosexuality without bias. In fact, since, according to homosexuals, they are the victims of widespread "homophobia" as the result of "outmoded religious prejudices", they are demanding that their behavior be defended and their rights affirmed *in America's classrooms*. In a curriculum that is supposed to be "value free", they want tolerance of homosexual behavior elevated to the level of a moral imperative.

For many years the homosexual organizations made minimal headway against people with good sense, who argued that school-based clinics and full-blown sex education courses were at best useless and at worst a subversion of family authority. Then, in one of the great and tragic ironies of our time, AIDS—a direct result of the sexual revolution and its rampant homosexual behavior—gave the sex educators the very opportunity they needed to ram through mandatory programs, not merely at the local level but on a statewide basis. They went to school boards and legislatures, waving a lot of frightening statistics and claiming to have a solution to this terrible problem that seemed to have arisen so suddenly.

"Since the disease is incurable and invariably fatal," they said, "the only way to stop the spread of AIDS is through education. And while you fools who believe in abstinence may not like it, you will have to teach your children about condoms, since they are going to have sexual intercourse, even though they know they are risking death."

Panicked by predictions of an "explosion" of AIDS into the heterosexual community and ignorant of the demonstrable failure of such education in preventing pregnancy, school officials all over the country bit the bullet and adopted emergency measures, in many cases despite the moral reservations they held personally. "I disapprove of such advice myself," some said, "but we have a duty to protect those young people who cannot resist the temptation to experiment. They must learn how to use condoms." They might have had second thoughts had they known that the homosexual organizations were just waiting for them to make this move, having quietly but effectively pressured publishers and professional educators to include highly positive treatments of homosexual experiences in their materials, offering these perverse practices as a legitimate and even desirable alternative to normal sexual behavior.

In order to clarify precisely what is going on in many of our churches and classrooms, I find it necessary to describe in some detail several examples of these curricular materials. In so doing I will try to avoid telling you more than you need to know. However, decent people cannot fully appreciate the danger of what is going on in our schools until they force themselves to look unblinkingly at the kinds of ideas and images to which their children are being exposed. We cannot ourselves be so squeamish that we avoid learning what is necessary to understand the forces now organized to alter our society. (Our squeamishness, remember, is what the homosexual activists are counting on.)

I will only add that these are not atypical courses used only in one or two schools. Nor were they produced by groups like the National Gay and Lesbian Task Force for their own training programs. One was produced and published by the Unitarian Universalist Association (known more popularly as the "Unitarian church") and has been in use for almost ten years. Its author boasted in a preface to the 1982 edition that it was being taught in schools and churches all over the United States, that Catholics were the largest purchasers among religious groups, and that 10 percent of their sales came from government agencies, including our armed services.

A second program, a curricular guide for setting up and conducting a course in human sexuality, was produced and published by the Episcopal church's Task Force on Human Sexuality in cooperation with the National Association of

Episcopal Schools. It was only out a short time, but it is being used all over the country, both by congregations and by church-related schools.

A third program was indirectly funded by the U.S. Department of Health and Human Services and distributed in the state of New Hampshire, before shocked local and state authorities ordered that it be recalled. As of this writing the American Civil Liberties Union is demanding that the program be circulated, despite the fact that both federal and local officials assert that it was produced in violation of their guidelines and regulations.

All three of these programs openly promote homosexuality and condemn anyone who believes that such deviant behavior is abnormal or undesirable.

I. *About Your Sexuality*, by Deryck Calderwood

About Your Sexuality, a multimedia program, was produced by the Unitarian Universalist Association (the Unitarian church), which currently distributes the materials. It is also distributed by Focus, Inc., a New York mail-order house that advertises other sexually explicit materials. Calderwood, who headed a graduate program in sexuality at New York University, died in 1986, some say of AIDS, though his wife maintains that he was the victim of cancer.

In a formal complaint lodged with the American Association of Sex Educators, Counsellors, and Therapists (AASECT), sex therapist Edward Eichel, who got his M.A. degree in sexology at NYU, charged that in a graduate workshop held in Holland, Calderwood had his male students disrobe and perform exercises in which they manipulated each other's genitals and gave each other "prostate examinations". Eichel claimed that in this workshop and in other phases of his graduate program, Calderwood was promoting homosexual behavior on the part of his students. As Eichel put it: "In view of the fact that Dr. Calderwood has recommended anal intercourse for males to experience 'role reversal', I feel certain that his objective was to stimulate interest in anal intercourse."[1] The same tendencies can be found in this curriculum, which sharply focuses on homosexual behavior, treating it in the same detail and depth as heterosexual behavior.

There is an assumption underlying such fine impartiality— an "egalitarianism" of sexual experience. All kinds of sexual behavior are equally acceptable, equally good, equally desirable. Likewise, no one has the right to object to anyone else's "preference". Several segments of Calderwood's course are devoted to the injustices suffered by "sexual minorities", and he suggests that students become actively involved in supporting homosexual rights. As part of a section on "sexual minorities", he publishes a "Dear Gay Caucus" letter and a "Homosexual Bill of Rights" as models for students to emulate.

Accompanying the Calderwood text are a videocassette and audiotapes. These materials are designed to be used with some portions of the printed curriculum and are likewise supportive of homosexual behavior. For example, the section "Lovemaking: Heterosexual, Bisexual, and Homosexual" is supplemented by an audiocassette on which three bisexuals express satisfaction in having intercourse with people of both sexes; then four homosexuals (one male and three females) say the following about their experiences:

Sharon: Shares her lesbian lovemaking experiences and how they enabled her to feel like a complete woman for the first time. (3 1/2 minutes)

Carole: Talks about how homosexual lovemaking is not just an experience of genital stimulation and orgasm but a

[1] In an unpublished letter to the American Association of Sex Educators, Counsellors, and Therapists, dated Apr. 26, 1987.

total relationship with the body and person of another human being. (6 minutes)

Eric: Talks about his early adolescent behavior and describes the range of feelings and variety of sexual activities that are part of his lovemaking with his lover. (12 1/2 minutes)

Ginny: Talks about falling in love with various girl friends during adolescence and young adulthood, of her early experiences of homosexual lovemaking, and of the good feelings she has about herself as a lesbian. (7 1/2 minutes)[2]

The videocassette portion is even more explicit than the printed and audio materials. The filmstrip is in color. Although it is composed of a series of still shots without sound, the photographs are clear and unambiguous, with the obvious intent of realistically depicting as much of the subject matter as possible, given the fact that there is neither motion nor speech.

The first segment depicts a black heterosexual couple engaged in normal intercourse. In this portion the genitalia are not exposed, but in the next segment, involving a white heterosexual couple, genitalia are photographed at close range. This couple is shown having normal intercourse, oral intercourse, and anal intercourse and performing oral-anal acts.

Next a male couple is shown in oral intercourse and anal intercourse and performing oral-anal acts. Then a female couple is shown in oral intercourse, performing oral-anal acts, and also using a dildo (an artificial device inserted into the vagina).

I repeat that all of these acts are photographed in color — and the activities are rendered in perfect clarity. Edward Eichel said that the young people performing these acts were Calderwood's students.

[2] Deryck Calderwood, "Lovemaking: Heterosexual, Bisexual, and Homosexual", in *About Your Sexuality* (New York: 1983), 10–11.

The course is specifically designed for children in the seventh and eighth grades, though *Sexuality Today* claims that it has been used in the fifth grade. Seventh- and eighth-graders are twelve to fourteen years old. Fifth graders are ten and eleven.

At the beginning of the course Calderwood stresses that these children must have the permission of the parents to enter the program. Once the program is under way, however, its proceedings are under tight security: "*Caution:* Participants should not be given extra copies of the form to show to their parents or friends. Many of the materials of this program, shown to people outside the context of the program itself, can evoke misunderstanding and difficulty."[3]

Why would anyone want to show such pictures to inexperienced youngsters, children just entering into adolescence? In a better time these would have been the years during which boys and girls tentatively began to date, to go to dances, to hold hands, to kiss and be kissed for the first time. Instead, they are being shown films of what jaded adults think they ought to know. Why? Because Calderwood says he wants them "to explore the meaning and significance of lovemaking to the human being"; "to provide accurate information to young people about heterosexual, bisexual, and homosexual lovemaking"; and one more mind-boggling idea: "*to make clear that sexual relationships with the same sex during youth are normal and do not necessarily indicate one's future sexual orientation as an adult*" (emphasis added).[4]

Note that there are two ideas embodied in this last statement, neither of them by any means a matter of fact, both presented as if they are generally accepted truths, something as verifiable as the multiplication tables. The first is that the homosexual acts depicted on the screen are "normal". Note that the text doesn't even say, "normal for those who are born homosexual". The meaning is clear—*homosexual relations in*

[3] Ibid., "How to Begin the Program", 3.
[4] Ibid., "Same Sex Friendships", 1.

youth are normal for all young people. The second idea is that you can "experiment" in youth with homosexual behavior and go on to a full, heterosexual adult life—a proposition that may be true only for some people.

Calderwood and others who hold these views are probably honestly describing life as they see it. Theirs is a warped world, unfamiliar and distasteful to most of us, and as we have seen in Chapter One, a world that many psychologists and psychotherapists regard as pathological, a shadow land in which normal becomes abnormal and vice versa. It is also a world unfamiliar and repulsive to the average teenager.

Calderwood knows that the natural tendency of many if not most young people will be to shrink instinctively from the sight of homosexual acts depicted on the screen. He adds a cautionary note for those who show these films: "You might compare any negative responses concerning the difficulty of accepting same sex lovemaking with the difficulty some people experience in watching a birth film the first time. It is a natural part of life, but we aren't used to seeing it. It may take some time to appreciate and enjoy the beauty of the experience."[5]

Reread this quotation two or three times and you will begin to discover what Calderwood is really up to. You will also see how he accidentally tips his hand. Note that while he says homosexual activities may seem repulsive at first ("negative responses"), if you watch them long enough, you may eventually "appreciate and enjoy the beauty" of these very acts. In other words, sodomy is an acquired taste, something you have to get used to. Yet he has also said, "sexual relations with the same sex are normal". So if they are normal, who do they produce these feelings of revulsion that have to be overcome by repeated exposure?

This basic contradiction is underscored in his poor choice of a comparison: homosexual intercourse is like childbirth—that

[5] Ibid., "Lovemaking . . .", 12.

is, "natural". In his effort to give sexual perversion an equal place with reproduction, he chooses the most natural and positive image he can think of—childbirth, the precondition of life itself. But built into this comparison is a self-defeating truth: homosexual intercourse never leads to the creation of new life, as heterosexual intercourse often does. Sodomy contributes nothing to the continuation of the human race. It is, in the eyes of nature, a useless, wasteful, and profoundly unnatural act. Calderwood's strategic error in bringing up birth reminds us of that truth.

So why does Calderwood want to condition young people to "appreciate and enjoy the beauty of" homosexuality? Why does he try to accomplish this end by exposing young people to scenes that they instinctively find repulsive? In one sense the answer to that question lies in Calderwood's understanding of sexuality. Whether or not he himself is a practicing homosexual or bisexual is less important than what he believes about the nature of sexuality itself, its basic meaning to human beings, its place in life.

It is important here to note that Calderwood does not say, as many homosexuals would now have us believe, that sexual behavior is instinctual or that it is invariably the result of hormonal imbalance. After the statement "genital intercourse is instinctual behavior for humans", he writes "*False*", citing quotations from several of the many (and often conflicting) studies on the subject: "There are no sexual instincts in man . . . human sexual behavior is entirely dependent on human conditioning. The individual's pattern of sexual behavior is *acquired* [emphasis in the original] in the context of his unique experiences and are in no sense innate or inherited." "Some mechanisms for sexual behavior are reflexive, but others develop only as a result of practice and learning. For example, a male does not need to learn how to fill his penis with blood so that it becomes erect, but he does need to learn how to copulate"; "*Without* specific sexual experiences, man outside of cultures—that is, so-called feral or natural man—or the extreme social isolate, does not generally engage in sexual behavior upon reaching puberty. There is no sexual instinct in man."[6]

In this segment of his program Calderwood goes against the current homosexual party line on the question of inherited sexual inclinations. He cites several studies to prove his point, studies the National Gay and Lesbian Task Force would just as soon forget. In taking this stance, Calderwood makes clear his reasons for including such detailed instructions on how to perform a variety of sexual acts: he is teaching our young people how they are to behave in such matters; he is doing society's job. Otherwise young people would never think of performing the perversions he is teaching.

Calderwood also makes another crucial point in a passage concerning the nature of homosexuality and homosexual behavior:

> It is important to distinguish between sexual behavior and sexual orientation. Homosexual individuals can participate in heterosexual intercourse (the majority of homosexuals have done so). Heterosexuals may also engage in homosexual activity (this is less common behavior) without affecting their basic sexual orientation. A lesbian may marry, raise children and throughout her life restrict herself to heterosexual intercourse, but at the same time be aware of her homosexual orientation. A homosexual male may also marry, raise children, and enjoy his family, but at the same time—fully aware of his homosexuality—may also engage in sexual relations with males. A heterosexual male may have sex with other males exclusively for extended periods of time (military service or prison) without affecting his desire for the opposite sex or his basic heterosexual orientation. A bisexual individual may often have more difficulty recognizing his or her orientation, may restrict sexual behavior to one sex for periods of time, and only later accept the sexual desire for both sexes as natural and right.
>
> The basic factor is not sexual behavior, but the meaning the sexual behavior has for the individual.[7]

[6] Ibid., "Resource Guide for Referenced Inventory of Sexual Knowledge", 15–16.

[7] Ibid., 1.

In this passage we find one of the chief messages of the homosexual movement, a message they believe the nation must accept before it can be "homosexualized": you can have any kind of sexual experiences you want to without significant alteration in your basic appetites. That means that the young people Calderwood wishes to influence could commit sodomy with frequency and still end up married and happily heterosexual. So whatever the students are taught and whatever they do won't really make a serious impact on their future lives.

As I have already pointed out, there are experts, including Kinsey, who believe precisely the opposite—that early experiences are crucial in determining what kind of sexual lives people will lead when they reach adulthood. Wardell Pomeroy, in his biography, says that Kinsey believed the nature of one's first experience could play an overriding role in determining future activity. Calderwood denies such a possibility in absolute and unequivocal terms.

What if he is wrong? What if this kind of sex education will actually promote homosexuality in our country by encouraging thousands of young people first to tolerate, next to try, then to adopt perverse behavior in the mistaken belief that it will have no effect on their future lives?

A recent biography of W. H. Auden reports that when the famous poet first began to experiment with homosexual behavior in college, he thought it was only a phase, something he would eventually outgrow. He was wrong, and the rest of his life was colored by his addiction to deviant behavior. A man of deep religious conviction in his later years, he might have led a normal life had he not believed homosexual experimentation was as harmless as Calderwood says it is.

How many schools nationwide are actually using the Calderwood program? It is difficult to obtain such information. However, the Unitarian Universalist Association has a very aggressive marketing program in place, and their representatives suggest it is being used by many institutions throughout the nation. And it is not the only program that takes this attitude toward homosexuality. Indeed, Episcopalians are now using a curricular guide that is derivative of *About Your Sexuality* and actually recommends the Calderwood materials as a resource.

II. *Sexuality: A Divine Gift*

Sexuality: A Divine Gift differs from *About Your Sexuality* in that it is more of an outline for a discussion group to follow than curricular material to be used in a classroom. *Sexuality: A Divine Gift* is also specifically religious in orientation, while Calderwood studiously avoids religious considerations except to mention in passing that religious beliefs often cause sexual inhibitions.

Despite these differences, the two programs have much in common: both have a permissive attitude toward unconventional or deviant sexual behavior, both advocate social tolerance of homosexuality, and both reserve their harshest language for those who believe that homosexual behavior is morally or socially wrong. Both programs also speak of the necessity to consider all opinions, all points of view; yet both dismiss anyone who takes a traditional view of such practices as homosexuality.

If anything, *Sexuality: A Divine Gift* is more outspoken in this regard, perhaps because it was written more recently, after homosexual activists had begun to dominate the media and to intimidate anyone who publicly opposed them. For whatever reasons, this program condemns those who believe that any kind of sexual conduct could be sinful, saying that such opinions are "judgmental".

As for homosexuality, the text argues that since sex is "a gift from God", it is therefore good by definition, whatever form it takes. In prescribing text materials and other resources to be chosen by the group, the text says:

The theology of the resource should present human sexual nature as a gift from God. Moral issues should center on the qualities of a sexual act, rather than the act alone. The attempt to use guilt to control sexual behavior should be seen not only as futile but also as a denial of the goodness of God's gift.[8]

And more specifically about homosexuality:

Look up "homosexuality" in the index of the resource. On the one hand, the sexuality-as-gift theology the church seeks to affirm views people with a same-sex orientation as people first, children of God, and members of Christ's body the church. Anglicans believe that they are people who can be as responsible as anyone else for loving, Christian behavior. On the other hand, the sex-as-guilt approach judges gay men and lesbian women in decreasing order of judgment as (1) people who choose to sin and can be saved by repentance, (2) people who are ill and can be cured, or (3) people who are handicapped or immature and who can be tolerated in the Christian community as long as they remain celibate. People with otherwise excellent views on sexuality are sometimes unable to look objectively at this particular subject. It is important not to use a teaching tool that gives a message of homosexuality-as-sin.[9]

As for the scriptural injunctions against sodomy, particularly in the writings of the Apostle Paul, the guide asks:

Does the resource use scripture in a positive manner? In the Anglican tradition, scripture is viewed as the living word of God revealing the divine relationship with people. The biblical story is one of release, exodus, liberation from slavery. It is the promise of new life in Christ for the Christian person. Does the source reflect this view, or does it present the Bible as a book of rigid rules to be followed on pain of punishment?[10]

The guide lists a number of quotations for discussion— some of them from Scripture—but none of the biblical material deals with sexual conduct outside of marriage. Even the words of Christ on such subjects as adultery and fornication

---

[8] [Episcopal Church] Task Force on Human Sexuality, *Sexuality: A Divine Gift* (New York: 1987), 88.
[9] Ibid., 88–89.
[10] Ibid., 89.

are omitted, to say nothing of the Law that He said He came to fulfill. In addition to the "positive" scriptural quotations, there are also a number of selections from sex manuals, homosexual polemics, and activist organizations like Planned Parenthood.

The first resource cited under "Other Suggested Titles" is Deryck Calderwood's *About Your Sexuality*.

Many Episcopalians have protested the introduction of this program into Episcopal schools and churches. They have pointed out that *all* things are "gifts of God", including language, and that the program properly condemns the misuse of language, while failing to acknowledge the obvious truth that other gifts of God, including sexuality, can likewise be misused.

As for the suggestion that those who condemn homosexual conduct are "judgmental", nowhere in the entire program is there the suggestion that homosexuals, like all the rest of us sinners, might be loved as brothers and sisters by those who disapprove of homosexual acts, or that suggesting other people are "judgmental" might itself be a form of "judgment".

This program caused a great deal of controversy within the Episcopal church, where some bishops demanded that it be withdrawn. Other bishops defended it, and the issue divided the members of that religious body as they prepared for their General Convention in July of 1988. At the convention the assembled delegates refused to approve *About Your Sexuality*, and it is in the process of reexamination.

III. *Mutual Caring, Mutual Sharing*

The squabble caused by *Sexuality: A Divine Gift* was less volatile than the uproar produced by the publication in April 1988 of *Mutual Caring, Mutual Sharing* (*MCMS*), a program that is obviously derivative of *About Your Sexuality*, probably because one of its chief architects was a former student of Deryck

Calderwood. *MCMS* was produced for the Strafford County Prenatal and Family Planning Clinic and was funded by a $161,000 Title X grant from the U.S. Department of Health and Human Services, a program designed to address the problem of widespread teenage pregnancy.

MCMS was patently offensive in several respects. It brought immediate protests from local and state officials, as well as from the Office of Family Planning in the Department of Health and Human Services, where Nabers Cabaniss, a deputy assistant secretary, demanded that local authorities stop the dissemination of the document. The program, it seems, had been originally funded under the "male involvement in family planning" category, designed to encourage males to be more responsible about preventing unwanted pregnancy. Instead, *MCMS*—which was prepared by Cooper Thompson, an activist in an organization called the Campaign to End Homophobia—was, among other things, a promotion of homosexual and feminist agendas.

In fact, in a prefatory page, the program acknowledges the principal contributions of Cooper Thompson, Chuck Rhoades (Calderwood's former student), and Bonnie Zimmer of the Feminist Health Center. In a final paragraph, the following appears: "Activities were adapted from the following sources: *About Your Sexuality* by deryck calderwood [*sic*]."

In an "Introduction to the Curriculum", the program gives as one of its goals "to foster an acceptance of the various sexual preferences and orientations of their peers, and an acceptance of their own sexual preference or orientation".[11] The Introduction also includes an acknowledgment (or boast) that the program is different and innovative in some respects: "We feel . . . that we have succeeded in approaching sexuality education in a new way, especially in terms of our emphases on gen-

[11] Cooper Thompson, *Mutual Caring, Mutual Sharing* (Strafford County, N.H.: 1987), 2.

der, sexual orientation, sexual coercion, and the assumptions about gender which form the theoretical basis of this work."[12]

While the language here is imprecise because of a heavy dependence on social science jargon, the general meaning is clear enough: what is principally new is their approach to homosexuality. Perhaps for this reason, like Calderwood they bar parents from participation, though they give a much more elaborate rationale for this exclusion:

> But after further conversations with sex educators and assessing our experience with teens and parents in other settings, we determined that it was unrealistic to expect parents to participate.
>
> Furthermore, we wondered if it made sense for the teens to have their parents participating when one of the primary developmental tasks for teens is to separate from their parents. . .
>
> Our working assumption until we are convinced otherwise is that it is unrealistic and even undesirable in most cases to include parents in this program.[13]

In response to the second paragraph above, may I say that teenagers' becoming independent of their parents in the conduct of their personal lives is one thing; developing values contrary to those taught by their own families is quite another. If this program—or indeed *any* program—has as its explicit purpose the "correction" of parental values and the establishment of "new norms", then it is propaganda rather than education, has no place in our public institutions, and should not be funded with taxes—some of which were paid by those very same parents.

This program differs in at least one respect from the other two—and particularly from *Sexuality: A Divine Gift*—in that it admits its biases rather than pretending to be fair-minded and objective. In a segment called "Assumptions and Biases about Sexuality Education", the program says the following:

[12] Ibid., 3.
[13] Ibid., 6.

We believe that sexuality is a natural and healthy process that spans all ages and that consensual sexual activity between two people is equally a natural and healthy process. There are, of course, good reasons for adolescents to delay the experience of penile-vaginal intercourse, e.g., questions about emotional readiness given the potential intimacy of this particular sexual act and the many complications that might result from a pregnancy. Other sexual acts, like oral-genital contact and penile-anal intercourse, may also be problematic because of the dangers of sexually transmitted diseases, and these may be magnified due to teens' generally poor use of condoms and inability to communicate with a partner about sexually transmitted diseases.

Despite these problems with some sexual acts, we don't take a stance against teens engaging in sexual activity per se. Rather, we assume that teens are sexually active even though their sexual activity might not take the form of penile-vaginal intercourse. (Unfortunately, being "sexually active" seems to have become synonymous in the public eye with penile-vaginal intercourse.)[14]

Note in this passage the tendency to warn against "penile-vaginal intercourse" (i.e., heterosexual intercourse) in absolute terms, while cautioning against "other sexual acts" that "may" be problematic only because of the risk of disease. "The potential intimacy of this *particular* act" (emphasis added) is reason for young people to delay heterosexual intercourse, but in the case of sodomy, the question is "problematic" only because of venereal disease. One presumes that other sexual acts between consenting minors, whether heterosexual or homosexual, are not "potentially intimate" or risky and are therefore acceptable. Indeed, the program says: "We don't pretend to be able to 'talk them out of' their sexual activity."

This passage is a carefully devised argument in favor of unnatural sex acts, with a built-in bias against normal intercourse—which, the program argues, is "potentially intimate". While most parents would agree with this evaluation of heterosexual acts between teenagers, they might have a hard time

---

[14] Ibid., 7.

admitting the permissibility of sodomy where there is no danger of sexually transmitted diseases. Yet the program is anything if not dogged in its defense of homosexuality:

> We chose to take an affirmative approach to sexual orientation in this curriculum because we, too, believe that the problem is a homophobic culture, not the behaviors of the gays, lesbians, and bisexuals in the culture. . . .
>
> Homophobia reinforces some destructive aspects of traditional sex roles by asserting that "real men" are attracted to women and are to behave in a manly fashion; to be gay or presumed to be gay is cast as being feminized, weak, and less than a man. . . .
>
> Parents' fears of a teacher "encouraging" homosexuality or bisexuality may make the teaching of a positive, affirming approach difficult, despite the fact that the parents' fears are not supported by the available research.[15]

How did this bias affect the way in which the program was conducted? Here are a few examples cited by the program:

> We set a groundrule [sic] early on that participants should refer to their sexual partners as "partners" or "sexual partners" rather than as "girlfriend" or "boyfriend." We did this as a way to provide some anonymity to those teens who might have a same sex partner and would feel unable to talk abut their experiences in the group. . . .
>
> In role plays, vignettes, or case studies, we always tried to include lesbian, gay, and bisexual characters in addition to heterosexual characters. . . .
>
> We made the assertion that gay and lesbian adolescents were perfectly normal and that their sexual attraction to members of the same sex was healthy.[16]

As if these activities and statements were not enough, the program introduces a new element into the dialogue about homosexuality and heterosexuality, one that neither Calderwood nor *Sexuality: A Divine Gift* broaches:

[15] Ibid., 9–10.
[16] Ibid., 10–11.

Lesbian and gay teens may be particularly confused and/or frightened about others' reaction to their sexual orientation (and they have every right to be) and so will only share this information in very rare circumstances. So it would seem unfair to allow heterosexual participants, *or more accurately those participants who believe they are heterosexual* [emphasis added], to state their sexual orientation in light of the experience of the gay or lesbian teen who does not feel safe to share their [*sic*] sexuality orientation. To make matters worse, a teen *who believes that they* [*sic*] *are heterosexual* [emphasis added] may declare their [*sic*] sexual orientation by a denial that they [*sic*] are gay or lesbian and perhaps make disparaging remarks about gays and lesbians in the process.

One way to solve this dilemma is by having a groundrule [*sic*] that no one should state their [*sic*] sexual orientation.[17]

In addition to the enormous alterations made in the teaching of this curriculum in order to accommodate homosexuals, note the italicized phrases, in which the program speaks of "lesbian and gay teens" on the one hand and "participants who *believe* they are heterosexual" on the other (emphasis added). In other words, homosexuals *know* about themselves, but heterosexuals may be deluding themselves. They may, in fact be homosexuals or bisexuals after all.

Such an insidious suggestion is guaranteed to disturb and confuse teenagers at this particular time in their lives. Whether intentional or unintentional, it disrupts the heterosexual youth community, causing these young people to have doubts about themselves and others in their group.

Even more disturbing is an exercise introduced later in the program in which the participants are divided up into male and female groups and told to talk about erections and menstruation. Then the groups get together and one listens while the other talks, and vice versa. The program states the following "Rationale and Objectives" for this exercise:

It may seem strange to discuss menstruation in the same breath with erections. We aren't trying to equate the two. For the purposes of the activity described here, we felt that it was important

[17] Ibid., 11–12.

to provide balance and so decided to include both. Quite honestly, our basic objective here was to expose the misogyny (literally hatred of women) that we believe young men have. The activity would serve our purposes if it only focused on menstruation, but we also believe that the participants might think it unfair if this were the case. . . .

. . . Men's attitudes [toward menstruation] border on disgust. Menstruation seems to represent for them the "weirdness," the mystery, perhaps even the evil nature and power of women.[18]

While these peculiar and highly subjective remarks are indicative of the paranoia that lies just below the surface of the more radical elements in both the homosexual movement and the feminist movement, they also serve to set young males against young females at just the time in life when they are learning to seek one another in a mature way. It's bad enough to pressure them into premature sexual relations as our society seems determined to do. It is worse to tell them that they are somehow *enemies*. The consequences of such confusion (and confused) advice cannot be beneficial to the promotion of healthy heterosexual attitudes. In some instances such advice might actually serve to promote homosexuality.

This course ends with an appendix that says, among other things, that "homophobia is the fear and hatred of gays and lesbians" as well as "the fear of being gay or lesbian"; in contrast

gay people are proud to be gay. They are proud of having learned the truth about themselves, despite societal prejudice and lies. Gay people are proud of their efforts to be granted their full civil and human rights. Gay people are proud of their homes, the families they have built and of the creative ways they lead lives.[19]

This statement was issued by the "Homophobia Task Force, National Organization for Changing Men" in 1984. Cooper Thompson, who drafted *Mutual Caring, Mutual Sharing*, is a key member of that organization.

---

[18] Ibid., 29–30.
[19] Ibid., "Definition of Homophobia", Appendix.

These three programs, although openly prohomosexual, are not the most offensive materials used in our schools and communities. That dubious distinction is reserved for some of the AIDS materials that have surfaced as the result of encouragement from health care officials. Much of this material comes directly from the homosexual community, which has sought and received massive funding for the development of educational programs directed at their own membership and those younger people who might join them. The results have been mixed. Some of the brochures and films have been intelligently produced, but much of the material is vulgar and obscene. When questioned about the propriety of such materials, the publishers invariably say it is the only kind of approach that will reach homosexuals—if true, a telling commentary on the nature of these sad people.

But the trouble is, this material too often is introduced into public schools by activist groups, such as the Western New York AIDS Program and the San Francisco AIDS Foundation. Sometimes homosexual teachers are the conduit for these materials. Sometimes they are approved by misguided principals and school boards, who have been told that young people routinely use obscene language and are involved in all sorts of sexual behavior despite the fact that a recent poll sponsored by Planned Parenthood and conducted by Lou Harris showed that only 28 percent of young people between the ages of twelve and seventeen had had sexual intercourse.

The assault on the sensibilities of our young people by pro-homosexual groups is illustrated by an AIDS brochure circulated, I am told, in Buffalo, New York, among eighth-graders. Published by the Western New York AIDS Program, it warns these junior high school students to avoid such behaviors as "anal or vaginal intercourse without a "condom"; "fisting"; "rimming (anal-oral contact)"; "oral sex, without a condom, with or without ejaculation in the mouth"; "sharing sexual aids (sex toys) such as dildoes or vibrators"; "poppers (amyl or butyl nitrates)"; "watersports; urine on unbroken skin is probably safe, but if it enters any opening, there is some risk".

In contrast, among the "Safe Sexual Activities" the brochure commends are "mutual masturbation, jerking off, manual stimulation"; "anal or vaginal stimulation/penetration with dildoes, fingers, etc."; "costumes and playing dress up"; "talking dirty, ('phone sex' is 100% safe!)"; "be creative, enjoy adding new things into your sexual play, try jello, whipped cream, pudding, wine, fruit, or fabric, feathers or other new textures that provide interesting tactile sensations"; and finally, "limiting your number of sexual partners reduces your chances of coming into contact with a number of STD's. Unless you engage in totally safe sexual activities; then you can have as many partners as your schedule allows!"

This brochure—entitled "AIDS: Prevention and Safer Sex"—is, in many respects, typical of the kind of materials being prepared by homosexual groups nationwide. The San Francisco AIDS Foundation, for example, has copublished a tabloid newspaper called the *Hot 'n' Healthy Times*, which features pictures of naked men putting on condoms and performing acts of sodomy. In addition, there are detailed descriptions of explicit sex activities rendered in four-letter words, which, according to those who produce these materials, are calculated to "eroticize" the use of condoms and as a consequence reduce AIDS and save lives.

Another piece of literature distributed by the San Francisco AIDS Foundation is a pink brochure called "Can We Talk?", which repeats much of the advice to be found in "AIDS: Prevention and Safer Sex", though using Anglo-Saxon words to describe sexual acts and parts of the body. After a group of women in Los Angeles began to protest, the Board of Supervisors for Los Angeles County schools passed a resolution condemning the brochure, but it still finds its way into the hands of young people throughout the state of California.

The influence of the San Francisco AIDS Foundation is not limited to California. The national hot line of that organization is listed in the *Surgeon General's Report*, which has been mailed to millions of Americans. Consequently, many people around the country—some of them young people—have called this homosexual organization to ask for information on the disease.

The same is true of the Gay Men's Health Crisis in New York City, which is also recommended by the *Surgeon General's Report*. In fact, the Gay Men's Health Crisis has been heavily funded by government sources, including the city of New York and the U.S. Department of Health and Human Services. In 1987 they were one of only six private recipients of federal AIDS grants, theirs a whopping $674,679, more than any of the other five, including Memorial Sloan Kettering.

Some of the educational materials they have produced are not only obscene but also recommend extremely high-risk behavior to homosexuals, behavior even denounced by the Surgeon General. For example, they published a series of six comic books, billed as "educational", which depict acts that most Americans have never heard about, much less performed.

One comic is a series of frames in which a leather-jacketed man first urinates on another man, then masturbates and ejaculates on him. This activity, which takes up eight animated frames, is described as "safe sex" and therefore becomes "AIDS education".

A second comic depicts two young men who engage in anal intercourse after fixing a leaky faucet. In one of the eight frames one young man puts on a condom. Again, the material qualifies as "educational" because of the presence of the condom.

(When this material came across my desk, I was so outraged that I sponsored a bill in the House to prohibit the use of federal funds for educational projects or materials "that promote or encourage, directly or indirectly, homosexual sexual activity". My friend Jesse Helms brought the same bill before the Senate. It passed in the House by a vote of 368 to 47 and in the Senate by a vote of 92 to 4. In conference committee, however, several conferees, obviously under heavy pressure from the homosexual activists, went against the instructions of their colleagues and removed the words "or indirectly", thereby introducing considerable leeway for circumventing the intentions of both houses of Congress.)

Homosexual activists have not restricted their invasion of American education to curricula and other printed materials. They have also demanded the right to establish homosexual organizations on campuses in order to further their interests and promote their sexual activities. At some of our colleges there are homosexual fraternities and sororities, as well as avowedly homosexual clubs. They actively recruit students. They demand and receive coverage in student newspapers. They wring concessions and money out of administrations. And when they encounter resistance, the full weight of the homosexual establishment swings in behind them.

A case in point is Georgetown University, a Catholic institution located in Washington, D.C. Because the Catholic Church has maintained its opposition to sex outside of marriage, despite the dissent of some priests and bishops, Georgetown University banned homosexual organizations from the campus, refusing either to recognize them or to provide them with funding. As soon as the university took this stand, the homosexuals filed a lawsuit.

The homosexuals made their case on the fact that the D.C. government had passed a "Human Rights Act" that, among other things, prohibited discrimination because of "sexual orientation". Georgetown based its defense on the First Amendment, arguing that their refusal to allow homosexual organizations on campus was an affirmation of traditional Church beliefs and that no local law could override the university's constitutional right to make school rules consonant with those beliefs.

After seven years of litigation, which the well-funded homosexuals could afford more easily than the university, the District of Columbia Court of Appeals ruled in favor of the homosexuals. The university asked the Supreme Court for a delay in implementing the decision while they decided whether or not to appeal. After Judge Rehnquist had granted them a short stay, however, the entire Supreme Court ruled 7 to 0 to deny their request.

As a consequence of this decision, on February 16, 1988, the student "Gay Association" held its first official meeting at the Georgetown University Law Center. According to the *Washington Blade*, a homosexual newspaper, "the event drew only about two dozen people". The *Blade* also announced that the university had agreed to give the group $3,740 to fund its activities. Shortly thereafter the university announced that it would not appeal the decision. So the homosexuals had won a great victory over the Catholic Church and indeed over all churches and synagogues that still believe in traditional morality.

What is significant about the Georgetown case is the fact that a city, state, or federal legislature can force a Church-related educational institution to fund activities that are contrary to its religious beliefs—provided those activities are homosexual. This decision has terrible implications for religious freedom in America. We can only hope that the Supreme Court itself will soon strike down this decision and substitute for it a reaffirmation of a religious body's right to maintain institutions that teach traditional Judeo-Christian values by example as well as by word.

But if you think the homosexual activists are content with establishing a beachhead in institutions of higher learning, you underestimate them. They have also begun to promote their attitudes and practices on high school campuses, in some cases with the full cooperation of administrators and school boards.

An outstanding example is Project 10, developed at Fairfax High School in the Los Angeles Unified School District. According to this club's own literature, "The target group consists of students who self-identify as gay or lesbian or students who express conflicts over sexual orientation."

Virginia Uribe, who started Project 10, is an avowed lesbian who is also a science teacher at Fairfax High. Her name has appeared frequently in newspapers, and she is invited to speak at various civic organizations in behalf of her "pilot program", which has won the approval of the principal, board members, and members of the West Hollywood community. Its financial supporters, or "friends", have included Christian clergymen, rabbis, civic leaders, and at least one nationally known figure—Paula Van Ness, who was at one point director for the National Information Campaign, National AIDS Information/Education Campaign, of the Centers for Disease Control.

In a recent letter thanking the many people who have made donations for Project 10, Virginia Uribe reports just how far the organization has come in its efforts to promote homosexuality: a library of "gay and lesbian literature" of over 500 books; the distribution of over 3,000 pamphlets offering information on "the special needs of gay and lesbian youth" to every junior and senior high school in the district; an essay contest "entitled 'Homophobia and Racism—A Common Thread'," with a cash prize; AIDS education, with their own noon seminars on "Sex in the Age of AIDS"; and cash awards at the end of the year for "those students who have demonstrated by their actions a commitment to lesbian and gay rights".

The letter ends with this paragraph: "Thank you once again for being a 'FRIEND' of PROJECT 10, and for sharing my hope that someday equality will include our lesbian and gay children."[20]

Incidentally, students are not the only people on campus for whom there are homosexual organizations. In New York City the Gay Teachers Association has been active for more than a

---

[20] Virginia Uribe, in a letter sent to "Friends of Project 10".

decade and affirms a number of "rights" that they are actively pursuing in the classroom. Among these "rights" are:

- "To educate all people about the outstanding contributions of gay writers, gay painters, gay historians, gay psychologists, sociologists, philosophers, and a host of other gay people who have invested their talents in the culture of a world society."

- "The rights of gay students to non-judgmental information and counseling."[21]

They also listed the following demands:

- "That the board of education include in the preamble of its contract with our union the phrase 'sexual orientation' in its listing of non-discriminatory practices."

- "That the board and unions work with us to establish a curriculum for teachers and students which would present a true picture of gay people, and to work with us to see that derogatory and inaccurate information be removed from any materials used in the educational system."

- "That the principle of academic freedom be supported for gay teachers so that they need not fear affirming their sexual preference nor fear correcting misinformation which might occur in or out of the classroom."[22]

This list of "rights" and "demands", published over ten years ago, is outdated. Much of what these teachers are affirming is now a matter of public policy in schools around the country, sometimes in conformity with local "gay rights ordinances", sometimes because administrators are in sympathy with homosexual pressure groups or are afraid of them. Thus homosexual teachers enjoy special protection, homosexuality

---

[21] From a flyer distributed in Albany, New York, July 8–10, 1977.
[22] Ibid.

is taught as "normal" and "good", and antihomosexual literature has been purged from school libraries.

As I noted at the beginning of this chapter, over thirty states have mandated some kind of sex education in the wake of the AIDS epidemic. Some of these states (e.g., Oklahoma, Alabama, and North Carolina) have put in programs that stress abstinence and traditional values. Others have allowed a greater leeway, and some have even endorsed programs that promote sexual experimentation and homosexuality. Since schools are largely under the control of local authorities, these prohomosexual programs must be addressed at that level. Parents must be concerned with what is going on in their local high schools and junior high schools. They must go to local principals and school boards and ask to see curricula and textbooks. (In most states such materials must be made available to the public under a "Freedom of Information Act".) If parents don't reclaim the public schools from the ideologues and activists of the left, then they may live to see their children's lives ruined by a new and irresponsible sexuality that runs contrary to everything we have believed in as a nation.

There are a number of groups determined that traditional morality will be destroyed by the end of this generation—and one of the most powerful of these is the homosexual movement. Their reasons for interjecting themselves into the education of our young should be obvious.

CHAPTER SIX

AIDS and Public Policy

For the past two years AIDS has occupied an increasingly important place in the American consciousness. In fact, today the American people regard the disease as the greatest single health problem in the nation. Certainly they are right. The number of cases is now increasing at an alarming rate. The number of dead continues to keep pace, despite new medications that seem to retard the progress of the disease. And there is growing evidence that the virus has made its way into the heterosexual community, though currently we don't know to what degree. (A recent study released by the Hudson Institute[1] suggests that there are almost twice as many cases of undetected AIDS in the United States as the Centers for Disease Control has projected, and that many of these cases will be found among heterosexual teenagers.)

Other experts (e.g., New York City Health Commissioner Stephen Joseph) have suggested that there may be fewer homosexual cases than previously estimated, but only because there seem to be fewer homosexuals than previous estimates indicated. But even this ray of hope cannot encourage us in the wake of increased numbers of reported cases and mounting death tolls. Virtually everyone is in agreement on one point: things are going to get much worse before they get better.

But why this grim prediction? Or, to put the question in even more pertinent terms, why have we allowed this disease to rage out of control, when we first diagnosed it almost a decade ago in no more than a handful of homosexuals? The answer to this question can be found in the attitude adopted by

[1] Kevin Hopkins and William B. Johnston, quoted in *Hudson Institute Report* (Fall 1988), 3-4.

187

answer to this question can be found in the attitude adopted by the homosexual leadership and the enormous influence that this small group has exerted on public policy at every level.

Clearly, from the outset AIDS has been a primary threat to the American homosexual community. Indeed, when the disease was first diagnosed in this country, it was probably confined to that particular segment of the population. Had public health officials quickly and effectively adopted traditional methods for dealing with sexually transmitted diseases, there would have been no AIDS epidemic and tens of thousands of people now dead would still be alive—most of them homosexuals.

But the homosexual activists—the officers and members of organizations like the National Gay Task Force—were intent on advancing a "gay rights" agenda and consequently made it difficult for indecisive public officials to root out the disease.

In a very real sense the homosexual community was faced with a choice at the moment AIDS first appeared in this country. They could either insist that they be allowed to continue their sexual practices undisturbed by public health officials, or they could submit themselves to the restrictions and procedures historically employed in treating sexually transmitted diseases and give up the idea of absolute sexual freedom, at least until the disease was eradicated. They chose to defend and advance their sexual revolution, even though to do so meant to risk the lives of tens of thousands of their own constituency.

It is true that the choice did not seem so obvious and so absolute at first. Only later, when the spread of AIDS had already reached epidemic proportions, could they fully understand the threat that uncontrolled and unmonitored sexual intercourse posed to the very survival of their community. Yet even then they chose to risk death rather than to accept discipline. With few exceptions the leaders of the homosexual movement have continued to fight every proposal to identify AIDS carriers and to curb dangerous behavior. Their attitude is clear: Give us liberty and give us death!

Let me illustrate what I mean. In San Francisco, where the AIDS virus was particularly prevalent, the homosexual bathhouse was a central gathering place for the most promiscuous homosexuals, those who engaged in countless sex acts with multiple partners. Some men had as many as ten sexual encounters in a single night, and in some cases their various partners numbered in the hundreds over the period of a year. At these bathhouses every conceivable perversity was practiced, but particularly anal intercourse, the most dangerous of all homosexual behaviors. A man would lie naked on his stomach, a can of vegetable shortening beside him, and wait for some stranger to enter. He would turn his head and nod, and the stranger would sodomize him. Typically, no conversation would take place, and the stranger would quickly leave. Then another would enter. And another. Such scenes would be taking place almost around the clock in the homosexual district.

Yet when San Francisco authorities tried to shut down the bathhouses as a health menace, the homosexual leadership hauled them into court and won an injunction to keep the bathhouses open—thereby ensuring that the AIDS virus would be passed from man to man in increasing numbers. Many California bathhouses are still open and are still the breeding grounds of the AIDS epidemic. Even today after a law was finally passed forbidding bathhouses, the suggestion that the bathhouses should be closed is met with stern opposition.

The same is true of other traditional health measures. Homosexual spokesmen insist that once-standard public health practices such as testing and contact tracing are foreign to the idea of freedom. Surprisingly, many commentators and public officials accept this version of American history without investigating its validity.

In fact, for generations the American public health community has routinely tested people for syphilis. At one time, most states mandated premarital testing, and many hospitals automatically tested all people entering, for whatever reason. In addition, during the late 1930s and early 1940s there was widespread testing in American industry involving literally millions, testing by federal agencies, testing by states (everyone between fifteen and fifty in Alabama), and testing by the Selective Service of all draft registrants during World War II (tens of millions of young men). The result of this antisyphilis program: hundreds of thousands of cases were diagnosed and cured, and the number of total cases was reduced to a fraction of what it had once been. (It is ironic that following the discovery of penicillin, many of these public health measures were relaxed or abolished, and now infectious syphilis is on the rise and has once again become a serious health problem.)

But in the past the health care community did not confine its activities to mere testing. They also reported cases of syphilis to public health departments and traced all sexual contacts of the infected patient, informing them of their risk, testing them, and also taking their recent sexual histories in order to identify additional infectious people. Almost every physician over fifty remembers such policies, even if they are no longer in force. Perhaps this is why an *MD* magazine poll revealed that a great majority of practicing physicians disagree with their colleagues in the U.S. Public Health Service, who have taken the homosexual position in arguing against routine testing and contact tracing for AIDS.

Of course, the homosexual leaders have argued that routine testing and contact tracing serve no useful purpose in dealing with a disease for which there is no cure. "Who cares if he has been infected with the AIDS virus?" they argue. "Better not to know, if you're going to die anyway." As noted in Chapter Three, this attitude was preached by the Reverend Troy Perry to his UFMCC flock, the largest homosexual organization in the country. As Troy explains it, he does not want his members to be additionally burdened with the knowledge that they are HIV infected when they already have enough troubles to weigh them down.

No argument better illustrates the psychological warp of the homosexual community, its intense and overarching self-preoccupation. This viewpoint is perfectly valid *as long as the only person you consider is the homosexual with AIDS*. But what about his future sexual partners? Don't they deserve every consideration that society can reasonably afford them? Isn't it valid to assume that at least some of the homosexuals who find themselves HIV infected will refrain from further sexual liaisons? Or restrict sexual activities to less-risky behavior? Or at least inform a prospective partner of the infection so that both people involved can make a realistic assessment of the dangers inherent in the sex act? Few husbands would want to submit their wives to the danger of infection if those husbands knew they were AIDS carriers. I would like to believe that many homosexuals would reject the self-centered policies of their leadership, if only because, in the end, they are not really defending the homosexual community but in fact contributing to its ultimate annihilation.

Let me put it another way. If all of the homosexuals who are now dying of AIDS could be given the opportunity to turn back the clock to 1981 and dictate public policy toward AIDS, would they order the bathhouses to remain open and allow the federal and state public health services to avoid testing and contact tracing at a time when only a few homosexuals were HIV infected? Or would they say, "Let's move to stop this thing in its tracks, so that a few years from now I won't contract the disease and end up in a hospice, my body covered with cancers, my lungs filling up with fluid."

Yet the situation has not changed. Those homosexuals who are still uninfected can join with those of us who want to reinstitute traditional health measures in order to save the remaining population from the virus. They can acknowledge that the measures we advocate are not only proven deterrents to the spread of sexually transmitted disease but also, if applied immediately, would be of primary benefit to homosexuals, because homosexuals are currently the chief transmitters and therefore the chief victims of the disease.

Yet those who advocate conventional health care measures are regarded by the homosexual leadership as "homophobes".

Ironically, anyone who genuinely hates homosexuals has an easy course to follow these days: simply give the "gay activists" everything they want. They are determined to lead their constituency to early graves. Their conduct in regard to AIDS is the best evidence yet that those psychologists who believe homosexuality is motivated by self-hatred are surely correct, because, with few exceptions, they seem determined to murder one another in a final death embrace.

Obviously, then, we must listen to someone other than the homosexual community if we are to adopt the best policies for meeting the AIDS crisis; and the most likely source of guidance is the U.S. Public Health Service, which has historically led the way in the prevention and containment of contagious disease. Yet, as already noted, such federal authorities as the secretary of Health and Human Services and the Surgeon General have not acted in the wise tradition of their predecessors. Instead of applying such proven methods as testing and contact tracing, they have been the chief opponents of these measures.

Indeed, the Surgeon General, Dr. C. Everett Koop, has become the adopted grandfather of the homosexual movement; and his 1986 *Report*, which supports the homosexual view of AIDS, is still being circulated by the U.S. Public Health Service, even though Dr. Koop himself has taken back some of his most important pronouncements in the light of emerging and contradictory evidence.

For example, Dr. Koop says that the use of condoms is a "measure" sufficient "to safely protect you" from the HIV virus, even though your partner is infected by the virus.[2] At the time he issued this report, some of us warned that well-known studies of condoms showed a 10 to 18 percent failure rate in the prevention of pregnancy and that at least one study published in Britain indicated a failure rate of up to 50 percent in anal intercourse. But for a long time he refused to acknowl-

[2] C. Everett Koop, in *Surgeon General's Report on AIDS* (U.S. Department of Health and Human Services: 1986), 17.

edge that his *Report* had overstated the efficacy of condoms or that other statements were likewise questionable in the light of later medical data. He stubbornly refused to admit that he had made a terrible mistake. Recently, however, he has confirmed that anal intercourse is dangerous, even with a condom, that he never intended his *Report* to suggest otherwise, page 17 notwithstanding.[3]

Yet the time has long passed when Dr. Koop and Dr. Bowen should have admitted their error or else removed themselves from their positions of authority. It has become clear that their policies have been wrongheaded and danger-ous. The public can now make this judgment in the face of emerging evidence regarding the failure of the so-called safe-sex approach to AIDS.

The first evidence came in a study conducted by Dr. Mar-garet Fischl of the University of Miami. Dr. Fischl, monitor-ing married couples where the male partner had AIDS, reported that after eighteen months of condom use, three of eighteen previously uninfected women had contracted the virus from their husbands. The failure rate, then, was about 17 percent over a year and a half. Not a very good figure to use in proving Dr. Koop's categorical assertions.

Early in 1987, the FDA began to look more closely at the condom industry as the result of the Public Health Service statements stressing their efficacy. At a time when Dr. Koop was saying that condoms were adequate "to safely protect you from the HIV virus", the FDA was telling my researcher that they didn't know how effective condoms were in preventing disease, that they could not specify the degree to which current testing procedures could answer such a question.

We discovered that the mechanical test the condom industry used—taking random samples, filling them with water, and seeing whether or not they leaked—allowed a failure rate of up to four condoms per thousand. That meant that in every 250

---

[3] Allan Parachini, *Los Angeles Times* (September 22, 1987).

condoms you might well find one that was punctured or broken, allowing sperm or the HIV virus to penetrate. These odds don't seem to bear out the promises of Dr. Koop's page 17, at least not over a long-term relationship.

But remember that 1 out of 250 was the permissible level of failure in the industry-administered test. When the FDA moved in to make certain that the industry was living up to those standards, they found out something very disturbing: about 20 percent of the condom batches—approximately one-fifth—*didn't even measure up to the standards.* So they had to recall literally millions of condoms, almost two million in one batch.

At this point some of us became concerned, and so did some reasonable people in the Department of Health and Human Services. The public was also nervous, since the FDA released the news of the condom recall to the general public. As a consequence of this growing concern, the National Institute of Child Health and Human Development (NICHHD) commissioned a study, to be carried out at UCLA and USC, that would attempt to answer the essential question: Do condoms really prevent AIDS?

In this study, the pregnancy figures of the past would be discarded. No one would rest with the knowledge that water would not squirt through a tiny hole. One phase, we were told, would involve attaching an electronic charge to an HIV virus and then seeing if it could penetrate a latex membrane. Another phase would involve monitoring two groups of human subjects, one using condoms, one without—or so the later reports would say. Very little about the mechanics of the study was revealed, only that it was intended to clear up doubts about the degree to which condoms could protect against HIV.

But it seemed as if the study was doomed from the beginning. First, the condom industry began to pressure the NICHHD to issue a "stop-work order" and shut down the project. The *Los Angeles Times* reported that the condom manufacturers were "motivated by industry concerns that the research might conclude that no American-made condom is currently able to consistently prevent the spread of AIDS".[4]

While the industry disputed this explanation, it demanded the following:

- That the UCLA-USC researchers use only those standards used by the condom makers themselves.

- That the Los Angeles study be forbidden to use more rigorous standards used by the International Standards Organization, a worldwide group of agencies. (The research team had wanted to test two European condoms, which conformed to ISO standards and which the researchers believed might be superior to American condoms in preventing HIV infection.)

- That if the study uses ISO standards, American manufacturers should be allowed to supply selected batches of condoms "especially screened for this". (The team had planned to use prophylactics purchased from retailers to be sure they were getting a representative sample of what was actually being used.)

- That researchers should test condoms only by filling them with water and not by inflation or by an electrical resistance test, two methods seen by some researchers as more reliable than the water test.

The principal investigator at UCLA, Dr. Roger Detels, wrote a letter refusing to allow condom makers to supply the products for testing, and the industry replied, asking that the study be discontinued until their other demands were considered. But the researchers went forward with their work.[5]

That was in August of 1987. In late January of 1988, the study again made the pages of the *Los Angeles Times*. This

---

[4] Alan Parachini, *Los Angeles Times* (Aug. 28, 1987).
[5] Alan Parachini, *Los Angeles Times* (June 27, 1988).

time, in violation of their own secrecy procedures, the UCLA researchers informed the FDA that they had discovered a batch of condoms so failure prone that they needed to be taken off the market. The discovery had first been made in November. The FDA had been informed, and the agency had in turn contacted the manufacturer, who reported that the entire batch had already been sold to unsuspecting customers. Yet in January of 1988 the researchers still found the same defective condoms on the shelf. These "rogue condoms" were so bad that some broke when they were being removed from the package, while others burst even before they were inflated to the required pressure.

This incident again suggested the degree to which the Koop endorsement of condoms was based on ignorance. As a matter of fact, in the *American Journal of Public Health* Paul Feldblum and Judith Fortney were saying that the scientific evidence to support the Public Health Service's campaign to promote condoms "isn't strong". "While use of condoms or spermicides is unlikely to be harmful," they wrote, "there is the potential for harm if their use is substituted for abstinence, monogamy, or good judgment." When asked about the implications of this article, Feldblum said, "We are not trying to kick the legs out from under that sort of program [i.e., the recommendation of condoms to prevent AIDS]. But we would like to see more information available before such [emphatic] recommendations are made. How many protections can be expected? How many cases of AIDS can we prevent [with condoms]? We really can't answer those questions."[6]

By July of 1988, the federal government had stopped trying—at least as far as homosexual intercourse was concerned. The National Institute of Health withdrew support from the UCLA-USC study. Why? Because, according to a *Los Angeles Times* story, there was "concern that the chances of trans-

---

[6] Joseph Carey, *U.S. News and World Report* (Oct. 19, 1987).

mission of the virus were made unacceptably great by the high prevailing infection rates, combined with the risk of condom failure".

As Dr. Jeffrey Perlman, chief of contraceptive evaluation for the NICHHD, explained it, "In a low-incidence area, you could say that condoms are almost foolproof. In a place like L.A., in the gay community, one would really be talking about delaying infection rather than preventing it. I certainly didn't feel that this was true a couple of years ago, but I do feel it is true now."

In other words, the federal government withdrew funding from the project because experts feared that those homosexuals who were using condoms in the study would be infected by the AIDS virus. As the *Los Angeles Times* reported it, "Perlman told UCLA's Detels that the NIH now fears that the risks of condom failure and subsequent AIDS transmission to study volunteers were unacceptably high."

When the *Times* tried to contact Dr. C. Everett Koop, "who has consistently urged condom use for people unwilling to abstain from sex entirely", a spokesman for the Surgeon General said Dr. Koop was "on vacation and unavailable".[7]

So a little more than two years after the *Surgeon General's Report* was hailed by homosexuals and by the press, and less than three months after the Department of Health and Human Services mailed a pamphlet, in which condoms were recommended, to every household, the federal government's AIDS policy seemed to be in shambles. You no longer heard responsible health officials talking about "safe sex" or even "safer sex". A stillness had settled over the Hubert Humphrey Building in Washington, D.C., where Dr. Koop wrote his report without help from another living soul and where he showed it only to Secretary Otis Bowen before he ordered it released to the world. No one was talking about the Los Angeles condom study or the implications it has for future federal policy.

[7] Alan Parachini, *Los Angeles Times* (Aug. 10, 1988).

Yet in the near future, someone in the federal government will have to reassess the entire AIDS program, withdraw the *Surgeon General's Report* from circulation, perhaps issue a "clarification" of the every-household mailer, and begin to plan and implement a positive program to prevent further spreading of the HIV virus. (Unfortunately, as the result of Dr. Koop's approach—the approach recommended by the homosexual leadership—people will probably die unnecessarily, convinced that, having used a condom, they are safe.)

What measures should this new policy contain, and how should it be implemented? If condoms are not, and never were, reliable, then on what *can* we rely? Are there things we are now doing that we shouldn't be doing? And are there things we aren't dong that we should begin to do? A number of us have been arguing for years that the present policy is flawed and dangerous. We have offered alternative plans, and they have been ignored. Now that the nation is without an AIDS policy, we offer these suggestions again, in hopes that whoever is in charge will listen to reason this time.

Here is my own list of priorities, with supporting evidence that these measures can form the basis for a sound AIDS policy. What I am recommending are steps that could have been adopted years ago and saved thousands of lives. But they can still be put into motion today, perhaps to save millions.

I. Widespread Testing

Widespread testing for the HIV virus is desperately needed, and for three basic reasons.

First, testing will ensure the best available medical diagnosis and treatment for infected persons. Recent studies indicate that early treatment slows progression of the disease, and one treatment is particularly effective. Animal studies strongly suggest that current drugs can effectively block the AIDS virus, especially if a person is treated soon after exposure to the virus. Antiviral agents, such as AZT, coupled with drugs that boost the immune system, have proven successful in stopping the progress of the HIV virus in attacking the immune system. Dr. Daniel Hoth, director of the National Institute of Allergy and Infectious Disease, has been so encouraged by these experiments that he was quoted as saying: "[T]his is the first time that I used the notion of a cure for AIDS." Dr. Ruth Ruprecht and a team at Harvard have shown that if mice receive AZT treatment at the same time they are infected with the Rauscher leukemia virus (a retrovirus related to HIV), the drug could prevent all the mice from being infected, while the infected mice who did not receive the AZT all died. In addition, the *New England Journal of Medicine* reported on July 23, 1987, that ARC patients on AZT for twelve months had a 94 percent survival rate compared with an 86 percent survival rate of patients who did not take AZT. (Researchers have also concluded that patients in the earlier stages of AIDS are much less likely to experience adverse reactions to AZT than people with full-blown AIDS.) So widespread testing would result in tremendous benefits for those who are infected with the virus, giving them a decided edge in the struggle to survive.

Second, a national testing policy would be beneficial to those who are not infected by the virus. For one thing, those who have engaged in high-risk behavior and who test negative would be reassured and could take steps to make certain they did not expose themselves again. But perhaps more important, if we are able to identify those who are HIV carriers, then we can persuade them to avoid exposing those who are as yet uninfected. Surely most people who discover they are carrying the virus will make some effort to spare others, particularly their spouses or long-term sex partners. So this knowledge alone will act as a significant deterrent to the spread of this dread disease.

And third, a substantial national sampling is needed if we are ever to determine just how many Americans are infected with the virus. No one knows the extent to which AIDS has spread throughout our increasingly promiscuous society. A couple of years ago CDC experts "guessed" that the total number of infected persons was about 1.5 million—a frightening figure. They came to this conclusion by estimating that the number of asymptomatic people carrying the virus was probably fifty times the number suffering from the advanced symptoms of the disease. At the time, the CDC had identified around 30,000 cases of full-blown AIDS. Today that figure is up to over 100,000, yet the estimate of asymptomatic carriers still stands at 1.5 million. We need to *know* the extent of infection in order to make plans for the future, particularly since a growing number of researchers are now saying that everyone who is infected will eventually die from the disease.

Currently experts disagree on their estimates, and the disparity is too great to ignore. Note what the following researchers say:

- Dr. Allan Salzberg, chief of medicine at the Veteran's Hospital in Miles City, Montana, has designed a computer model that uses current CDC data to predict that by 1990 — the time is short—there will be 490,000 cases of AIDS, over 400,000 new cases in two years. This model also predicts that by 1991, 263,000 people will have died from the disease and that by the year 2000 there will be 6.1 million cases, 20 million carriers, and 4.5 million dead. This magnitude of infection would produce a direct cost to society of $29 billion and an indirect cost of $129 billion.

- The Rand Corporation estimates that there could be as many as 750,000 cases of AIDS by 1991 and a total of 500,000 deaths.

- In *Crisis*, a recent study, Masters, Johnson, and Kolodny concluded that 3 million people are currently infected with the virus—twice the estimate of the CDC. In addition, they estimated that 1,600 contaminated blood samples may be escaping detection each year.

Perhaps the most widely debated epidemiological question is the extent to which AIDS has spread into the heterosexual community. The U.S. Public Health Service has estimated that 30,000 heterosexuals are currently infected. They base this figure on data gathered by the blood banks, by the army, and by researchers engaged in small-scale studies. But other experts disagree:

- A 1987 report by the U.S. Army indicates that .21 percent of active-duty members are infected with the AIDS virus. If that rate holds true for the general population of males between seventeen and fifty-nine, then we have approximately 149,000 cases of infection among low-risk heterosexuals.

- In Alameda County, California, health officials conducted secret AIDS tests in 1986 to determine the rate of public infection. The tests were conducted on 2,000 women applying for marriage licenses, visitors to local venereal disease clinics, and youngsters in Juvenile Hall. This sample indicated that .5 percent of the samples taken from women applying for marriage licenses contained AIDS antibodies—the same percentage found in female visitors to venereal disease clinics.

- Masters, Johnson, and Kolodny believe that 200,000 heterosexuals who don't use drugs are probably infected—an estimate nearly seven times higher than the CDC's. In their study of 800 volunteers—400 monogamous heterosexuals and 400 promiscuous heterosexuals—only one of the monogamous heterosexuals was infected by the AIDS virus (2.5 per thousand), while 7 percent of the promiscuous women (seventy per thousand) and 5 percent of the promiscuous men (fifty per thousand) tested positive.

Clearly, then, there is substantial disagreement among experts, and this disparity between estimates is not a minor squabble. We must know as much about current infection as we possibly can in order to prepare for the future. If these higher estimates prove to be accurate, then as a nation we are totally unprepared for the catastrophe about to overtake us, the magnitude of which is beyond current comprehension. We must drastically revise our long-term medical planning. We must quickly develop a fiscal policy for dealing with such enormous expenditures. And we must frame a legislative program that will cut our losses while at the same time guaranteeing that in a time of dire national emergency our nation can retain its traditional atmosphere of freedom and compassion.

Those who oppose routine testing also argue that voluntary testing will be just as useful. But voluntary testing has not worked. Less than 2.5 percent of HIV cases discovered in the military came to light as the result of "self-referral", and less than 2.5 percent were identified after admission to a clinic. That means that more than 95 percent of all HIV-infected cases in the U.S. Army were identified as the result of one of the army's mandatory screening programs.

According to Dr. Robert Redfield, an AIDS researcher at Walter Reed Hospital:

> Self requested testing is a discriminatory and limited approach, offering the opportunity to be tested only to those who are reached by education programs and who understand the importance and benefits of such knowledge. Routine testing provides equal opportunity to all. . . . Voluntary exclusion will allow the minority [who fear name-linked testing] to maintain access to [sexually transmitted disease] and drug rehabilitation clinics. This approach enables the majority of Americans to be informed of their infection status independent of education or social background. Because knowledge is so important to the control of the AIDS epidemic, we must maintain free and easy access to no-name-linked testing and counseling sites for the minority that opt out of routine testing programs.[8]

---

[8] Robert Redfield, Testimony before the Subcommittee on Health and Environment on Energy and Commerce (May 1, 1987).

If we are to have routine testing, then who should be tested? For reasons that will become apparent, I would suggest that the following groups be included in any comprehensive testing program.

A. PERSONS CONVICTED OF INTRAVENOUS DRUG USE, PROSTITUTION, OR SEXUAL ASSAULT

Such people should be tested to protect potential "customers", cohorts, and victims. We also need to determine the rate of infection among such groups in order to assess the need for greater law-enforcement efforts and additional legislation.

Intravenous (IV) drug users have been considered a high-risk group from the outset of the epidemic. Currently, they account for 17 percent of all cases, and another 8 percent are cases of male homosexuals who also use IV drugs.

Prostitutes have recently been singled out by the FDA as a "high-risk group", and for good reason. In a study conducted by Howard University, thirteen out of twenty-six prostitutes tested were found to be infected with the HIV virus. In a CDC study, researchers found that one out of nine prostitutes tested nationwide was an HIV carrier. A Miami study found 58 percent of all prostitutes tested were positive for HIV. These figures more than justify the classification by the FDA.

Persons convicted of sexual assault and related crimes should be tested because they have placed their victims in jeopardy. In addition, the results of these tests should be made available to the victim so that he or she will be reassured or else informed about infection in order to take all steps available to minimize the dangers involved. Currently, many states refuse to perform the HIV test on those convicted of sexual assault, and some states that do perform such tests will not release the results to victims. In my opinion, such a policy is shortsighted and inhumane and favors the criminal rather than the victim of the crime.

B. PERSONS RECEIVING TREATMENT OR SERVICES FOR FAMILY PLANNING, TUBERCULOSIS, DRUG ABUSE, OR SEXUALLY TRANSMITTED DISEASE

Persons receiving treatment or services for family planning have committed no crime, so why test them for HIV? Actually there is a good epidemiological reason for doing so. Evidence suggests that an increasing number of younger women will become infected with HIV, either as a result of IV drug use or through heterosexual transmission of the virus. Title X, a federally funded program, annually provides family planning services to 4.3 million sexually active women. Most of these women (about two-thirds) are below the age of twenty-five, many are members of minority groups, and 85 percent are members of low-income families. For this reason, Title X clients closely resemble the population of women thought to be at risk for HIV infection. Thus, in testing these women we can help those who are infected (see above) and at the same time learn more about this particular population of women in order to assess the spread of AIDs into the heterosexual community.

Persons receiving treatment for tuberculosis are more and more likely to be AIDS victims as well. Tuberculosis (TB) is the latest of the known diseases associated with the HIV epidemic. Unlike other opportunistic infections, however, tuberculosis is an airborne disease and seems to be contracted more easily than other opportunistic diseases. Consider the following facts:

- In March of 1987 the *Mortality and Morbidity Weekly Report (MMWR)* announced that the rate of tuberculosis in AIDS patients was more than 100 times higher than in the general population.

- Between 1985 and 1986 tuberculosis rates rose for the first time since records have been kept on the disease.

- Dr. Dixie Snyder, director of the Division of TB Control at the Center for Prevention Services, reported that 4.6 percent of AIDS cases have also been infected with TB.

- TB was found in 10 percent of the 1,094 AIDS patients in a Florida hospital.

- In a recent study of seventy-one patients in Dade Country, Florida, 31 percent were HIV positive, and in a New York State prison, 100 percent of TB patients who agreed to be tested were HIV positive. In fact, the largest increase of TB in the country occurred in New York City, where the rate jumped by approximately 50 percent between 1981 and 1986.

The heightened threat posed by tuberculosis is illustrated by the case of twelve Urbana nurses who tested positive for TB after caring for two patients suffering from both AIDS and tuberculosis. This outbreak, which occurred at the Carle Foundation facility, was described by a resident physician as an "epidemic".

This case illustrates the wisdom of testing all patients with tuberculosis for HIV as well. But there is also another reason: a positive HIV test can change the recommended treatment for TB. According to the American Thoracic Society, "The presence of HIV infection in a person with tuberculosis alters the management of TB and should make the physician alert for other opportunistic infections."

Persons receiving treatment for drug abuse, as noted above, are especially at risk for HIV infection and need to be diagnosed and treated for the AIDS virus, which is as deadly as a drug habit.

Persons receiving treatment or services for sexually transmitted diseases (STD) are also a high-risk group. It is estimated that a minimum of two million people annually are diagnosed with a sexually transmitted disease or treated for such a disease.

Several studies indicate that health officials may have underestimated the number of these people infected with HIV.

- A 1987 study of male visitors of New York City STD clinics revealed that 3.4 percent of heterosexuals who did not use drugs were HIV positive.

- A Baltimore study of 4,028 patients visiting STD clinics found that 5.2 percent were HIV infected (6.3 percent of the men and 3 percent of the women). The report said: "A disturbing finding of this study was that one-third of infected men and nearly one-half of infected women did not acknowledge any high-risk behavior, suggesting they were unknowingly infected through heterosexual conduct."

- A 1988 study in Fairfax County, Virginia, found an "alarming" number of HIV-infected heterosexuals who visited STD clinics. In a random sample of 215 blood samples from heterosexuals, 4.7 percent carried the AIDS virus.

These statistics indicate that persons being treated for STDs are not only at high risk for infection but in many cities may already be infected. It is crucial that we test this population as expeditiously as possible in order to determine the infection rate and begin intensive counseling about the potential for transmission.

C. PREMARITAL APPLICANTS

Premarital applicants are not any more at risk than other members of the population at large, but testing couples before marriage can be justified for two reasons.

First, a large number of couples seek marriage licenses each year, and therefore this test would serve as a good random survey of the magnitude of infection in the United States. The CDC estimates that there were approximately 2,495,000 marriages in the country last year. Assuming the number of people who married twice is negligible, we could have tested approximately 4,990,000 people and learned much of what we want to know about the dimensions of the AIDS epidemic. Such testing would be easily instituted and economical in those states that already require testing for syphilis and gonorrhea.

Second, the potential spouse of a person who has been exposed to AIDS has the right to know if that person is HIV positive. Such knowledge is essential to making decisions concerning sexual relations and procreation. Indeed, a major goal of premarital testing is to protect unborn children. Recently the mother of an AIDS-infected child was quoted as saying that she would never have married had she known her husband was infected. She said, "I do not regret having him and I would not have had an abortion, but doing this to a baby is like holding a gun to a child's head."

D. HOSPITAL ADMITTEES BETWEEN THE AGES OF FIFTEEN AND FORTY-NINE

Routine screening of this group over a one-year period would result in the testing of 37 to 39 million people and would provide the large base of statistical data necessary to determine the extent of the epidemic.

In the past, critics of this proposal have made the hyperbolic argument that the cost per positive test would run as high as $18,000, assuming that children and old people would be tested. But limiting the sample to this age group would reduce the cost to $150 per positive test, a genuine economy if we could determine the extent of the AIDS epidemic and at the same time identify and treat large numbers of AIDS sufferers.

The American Medical Association has recommended voluntary testing instead of routine testing, but such an approach has thus far proved unsuccessful. Consider the following examples:

- According to physicians at the Bellevue Hospital Center in New York, voluntary screening missed more than 85 percent of pregnant women infected with the deadly virus who were admitted to Bellevue between October of 1986 and July of 1987. Of the 1,192 samples tested for antibodies, twenty-eight were HIV infected. Thus, voluntary testing failed to identify twenty-four of twenty-eight HIV-infected mothers and their at-risk children.

- Similarly, in a New York inner-city hospital, twelve (2 percent) of 602 blood samples of newborn infants were HIV positive. Seven of the twelve seropositive mothers had risk factors, but the remaining five did not. The HIV seroprevalence rate in that hospital is several times higher than the rate for other diseases for which screening is already routine. The conclusion of hospital authorities:

> In our institution, self-reporting and physician interviews identified only 7 (58%) of the 12 potentially seropositive patients. Thus, if our physicians had followed the current recommendations of the CDC, asked patients about risk factors and recommended that those at risk be tested, five (42%) of the seropositive would have gone undetected.[9]

Many medical authorities disagree with the AMA and are taking steps to institute a more sensible testing policy. Despite pressure from the AMA and other groups, surgeons at the Medical College of Wisconsin initiated a policy of mandatory testing for surgery patients in October 1987. Dr. Robert Condon, chairman of surgery, said that "sometimes the right to privacy has to be counterbalanced against society's needs . . . the risks are low, but not zero." He went on to say that physicians in Wisconsin feel "it is appropriate to reduce the risk".

---

[9] Sheldon Landesman et al., "Serosurvey of Human Immunodeficiency Virus Infection in Parturients", *Journal of the American Medical Association* 258 (Nov. 20, 1987), 2701–3.

The policy calls for denying surgery to those who refuse testing, but so far no one has refused.[10]

In February 1988, Parkland Memorial Hospital in Dallas tested 709 emergency room patients without their knowledge. Approximately 1 percent tested positive for the HIV virus, and these were informed of the results. The AMA was swift in its condemnation of Parkland, stating that the hospital's conduct was unethical, but Parkland's president defended the tests, saying, "The only patients who were tested were severely injured and needed their blood drawn for other tests. Blood samples were coded to protect the patient's identity." He also added, "The AMA would be happier if we did not notify people who tested positive. We could let those people go and infect their loved ones but we feel obligated to the patients."[11]

One of the main reasons for testing hospital inpatients is to ensure that the infected receive proper diagnosis and treatment. Even Surgeon General Koop has recommended that all patients scheduled for major surgery be tested for HIV infection.

There are also good legal reasons for testing hospital inpatients. In Cambridge, Massachusetts, in January of 1988, a physician was found liable in what lawyers call the first AIDS malpractice case in the nation. A Middlesex Superior Court judge ruled that Dr. Kenneth Bernstein was negligent in his diagnosis of a female patient and in her treatment. The woman claimed Dr. Bernstein diagnosed her as having asthma when she really had AIDS-related pneumonia. The woman, Mrs. Elizabeth Ramos, was awarded $500,000, and her sons Christopher and Matthew were awarded $125,000 each.

---

[10] Unsigned story by Associated Press, "Chief Surgeon Says AIDS Testing to Continue" (May 9, 1988).

[11] Unsigned article, "Dallas Hospital Secretly Tested Patients for AIDS", *Washington Post* (Feb. 7, 1988), 146.

Finally, inpatients should be tested for HIV so that hospital personnel can be informed about the dangers they face. In view of the proven risk of transmission by blood, hospital personnel should know the infection status of all patients. Here are four cases to illustrate the need.

- In September of 1987, the CDC reported three cases of transmission to health care providers. In the first, a nurse held a catheter in place for a comatose AIDS patient with the tip of her ungloved finger and became infected with HIV. In the second case, a woman who had small cuts and eczema on her hands was infected while caring for a man in his home. The third case involved a woman who contracted HIV while caring for her child, who had been infected as the result of a blood transfusion.

- More recently, London officials called for the testing of all hospital patients before surgery after it was reported that a surgeon practicing at the Royal Devon and Exeter Hospital was infected with the AIDS virus when he performed surgery on a child in Zimbabwe.

In summary, let me say that we should have established a testing program of considerable scope when we first discovered the nature of the virus in the early 1980s. I am convinced that we would have done so had AIDS been a predominantly heterosexual disease. Routine testing has always been standard procedure in dealing with such infections as syphilis and tuberculosis. And it is important to note that when, during the Roosevelt administration, testing for syphilis reached its most intense level, the stigma of venereal disease was far greater than the stigma of AIDS or homosexuality today. To argue to the contrary is to admit a radical ignorance of the past.

Yet the homosexual activists, through a campaign of intimidation and misinformation, have convinced a large segment of the American population that there is something new and sinister about testing people in order to check a disease that has killed tens of thousands already and may kill millions before it runs its course. Somehow we must recover our good sense, if not our memory, and reinstitute the kind of testing program that helped to stamp out syphilis within the lifetime of millions of Americans.

II. Reporting

We must also institute a national policy of reporting HIV infection just as we report other communicable diseases, including full-blown AIDS. Every physician who diagnoses the HIV virus in a patient should be required to report the fact to public health authorities. Currently, every state has a law mandating that cases of syphilis and gonorrhea be reported. But only fifteen states—Alabama, Arizona, Arkansas, Colorado, Idaho, Michigan, Minnesota, Mississippi, Missouri, Oregon, Rhode Island, South Carolina, South Dakota, Wisconsin, and Wyoming—currently require the reporting of positive HIV results. There are several reasons why all states should require reporting of AIDS.

First, such a policy would allow us to obtain more accurate statistics on the numbers of people infected with the virus. Such knowledge is essential in assessing the magnitude of the epidemic and in making plans for meeting this crisis in the future. Thus far we have only scattered reports, some of them no more than fragmentary records. So our projections for the year 2000 are based on guesswork. Until we have a widespread testing policy, we will still know less than we should, but nationwide reporting of cases would be a start.

Second, a system of reporting would enable us to locate HIV-infected persons and counsel them about their condition. As noted above, recent studies indicate that early treatment may significantly increase the likelihood of retarding the progression of the disease and perhaps even halting it. Physicians or health authorities would also have the opportunity to recommend measures to prevent the transmission of the disease to loved ones. At the same time, they could establish a list of sexual contacts or people with whom the infected persons have shared needles, so that these, too, can be tested and counseled.

Third, medical researchers are beginning to develop treatments and even medication that can prolong the lives of AIDS victims. The sooner we can identify patients with AIDS, the sooner we can provide them with the latest medical information to assist them in surviving and maintaining as healthy a life as possible.

A number of medical authorities have subscribed to the policy of mandatory reporting. Among these are the following:

- On June 1, 1988, the National Academy of Sciences recommended that HIV infection (not merely full-blown AIDS) be declared a disease, because "it may be eventually amenable to treatment and patients will need to be diagnosed and treated as soon as possible". They also pointed out that "even asymptomatic persons are capable of infecting others".[12]

- The American Medical Association now supports anonymous reporting. However, in the same breath, they also recommend partner notification, a policy that suggests some compromising of anonymity.

- The Medical Society of the state of New York (MSSNY) recommended in February 1988 that reporting be "confidential" but not "anonymous", as the AMA had suggested.

- Dr. Jerome Schwartz, President of the New York Obstetricians and Gynecologists Medical Society; Dr. Francis McKee, President of the New York State Society of Surgeons; and the New York State Society of Orthopedic Sur-

[12] Institute of Medicine/National Academy of Sciences, *Confronting AIDS: Update 1988* (June, 1988), 82.

geons have filed a lawsuit against state Health Commissioner David Axelrod to force him to add HIV infection
to the list of communicable, sexually transmitted diseases.
This action would make HIV infection reportable.

- In their book *Crisis*, Drs. Masters, Johnson, and Kolodny
  endorse the concept of reporting. They state:

  We believe that [widespread] testing, reporting and contact tracing programs will do more on the balance to preserve civil rights
  than to weaken them. With adequate attention to the details of
  providing the maximum degree of confidentiality possible—
  both legislatively and in the administration of public health
  departments and testing laboratories . . .—we can keep disrup-
  tions of civil liberties to a minimum while significantly increasing our vigilance against a lethal disease that could prove to be
  the worst natural calamity of this century.[13]

- Dr. James Mason, director of the Centers for Disease Control, at a 1987 hearing before the House Subcommittee on
  Health and the Environment, said that "the reporting of
  both AIDS cases and infection would help us tremendously
  with understanding better the incidence and prevalence of
  this infection, and some states are reporting HIV positive
  tests and handling that very well".[14]

- Following Dr. Mason's statement, Surgeon General C.
  Everett Koop said for the record: "I agree with everything
  he just said."[15]

- Recently, the President's Commission on the HIV Epidemic recommended that HIV infection should be the statistical basis for reporting the AIDS epidemic.

Some opponents of mandatory reporting of HIV argue that
such a policy would force those in high-risk groups under-

---

[13] William H. Masters, Virginia E. Johnson, and Robert C. Kolodny, *Crisis: Heterosexual Behavior in the Age of AIDS* (New York: 1988).

[14] James Mason, Testimony before the Subcommittee on Health and Environment on Energy and Commerce (May 1, 1987).

[15] Koop, loc. cit.

ground, that they would no longer consult physicians who might obey the law, that leaders and public health officials have taken this line. The facts do not support such an assertion.

In order to clarify the issue, let's compare what has happened in the state of Colorado with what has happened in California. Colorado requires all physicians and laboratories to report every incidence of HIV infection to the state health department. California, in contrast, subjects physicians to criminal penalties if they tell anyone, including the state health department, about a case of HIV infection. So in which state has the most voluntary testing occurred?

In Colorado. The Colorado state department of health reports that thus far they have tested 6 percent of their population—a remarkably high number. And what about California, with the strictest confidentiality laws in the nation? California reports having tested only 1 percent of their population, despite the fact that two of the five major problem cities in the country are Los Angeles and San Francisco.

III. Contact Tracing

Once HIV carriers are identified through testing, it is important to begin contact tracing (or, as public health officials now like to call it, "partner notification"). This is traditional medical practice, particularly in the prevention of sexually transmitted diseases. Thomas Parran, Franklin Roosevelt's Surgeon General, strongly advocated the measure in his 1937 book *Shadow on the Land: Syphilis*, and throughout the late 1930s and 1940s it was standard procedure at the local and state levels. In fact, when cases of syphilis were diagnosed in federal clinics, the names of all contacts were taken and forwarded to local authorities for follow-up with testing.

Clearly HIV contact tracing is desirable for at least three reasons.

First, it provides epidemiological information of a specific sort. While routine testing can tell us how widely the AIDS epidemic has spread, contact tracing can more sharply define the manner in which the virus is communicated from one person to another: the kind of sexual activity involved, the frequency, the number of partners, the nature of the partners, and (most importantly) the network of infection produced by a single carrier. No information could be more useful in developing an educational campaign to warn noninfected persons against high-risk behavior.

Until now our pronouncements about the rate of transmission are at best speculations based on limited testing and the small amount of contact tracing thus far carried out. Were HIV contact tracing routine—as it has been with syphilis and even typhoid fever—we might be able to pinpoint the precise nature of risk in a variety of behaviors and also predict with a greater degree of accuracy the continued spread of the disease.

Second, contact tracing would be helpful to those sexual partners or needle sharers who are already infected with the virus. They could begin immediate treatment in order to retard the progress of the disease, and they could also make certain that they did not expose anyone else through continued high-risk behavior.

Third, those contacts who are uninfected could live their lives with a greater sense of well-being, knowing that they had been fortunate enough to dodge the bullet. By the same token, they might well reassess their own behavior, knowing they had been exposed to such a deadly disease and escaped the consequences.

Homosexual activists and some public health officials have consistently opposed contact tracing, arguing that it is a violation of the individual's right to privacy and that it is an ineffective and costly way to identify AIDS-infected persons. As far as I know, the courts have never ruled that contact tracing is unconstitutional; until they do, there is no "civil right" to infect others or even to remain ignorant of one's own infectiousness. The health of the public has always outweighed the individual's right to freedom of association, particularly if "association" means sexual intercourse with persons other than a spouse.

As for the argument that contact tracing is ineffectual, experience in several states seems to indicate otherwise, and even the CDC has admitted in principle to the efficacy of the measure:

- In Colorado, state authorities interviewed and tested 296 sexual contacts of HIV-infected persons. Out of that number, forty-five were HIV infected—a total of approximately 15 percent.

- In Idaho, fifty-nine partners were located and tested. The result: twenty-three, or approximately 39 percent, tested positive for HIV.

- In South Carolina, authorities tested sixty-eight sexual contacts who assented to the procedure. Of the sixty-eight, twelve proved to be seropositive, a total of around 18 percent.

- Virginia authorities traced and tested 318 contacts during a fifteen-month period and discovered that forty-four (14 percent) were infected with the virus.

- In a 1987 issue of *MMWR*, the CDC recognized the principle of contact tracing by saying that physicians should use confidential procedures to assure that the partners are notified.

Needless to say, contact tracing has *always* been a "confidential procedure". Even in the heyday of Thomas Parran, when the eradication of syphilis was the chief mission of the U.S. Public Health Service, the names of sexual contacts were never made public. Like private physicians, public health officials were bound by ethical codes, and there is no reason to believe that these codes were ever breached.

It is also obvious that infected persons *always* surrender the names of contacts voluntarily, though some patients may require more persuasion than others. The government has never employed force to discover the identity of sexual partners, and no one has ever advocated such measures. Most people, presented with the obvious benefits of revealing names, eventually do so voluntarily. Clearly, however, any individual has the option of refusal—and always did, whether the disease was syphilis, gonorrhea, or typhoid fever.

IV. The Restoration of Laws against Sodomy

According to legal historian Charles Rice, every state in the Union outlawed sodomy until 1961. These laws, as noted in Chapter Two, were based on ancient legal tradition and derived from our society's roots in the Judeo-Christian ethical and moral Tradition. Then, in the following twenty-five years, homosexual activists and organizations like the American Civil Liberties Union mounted an assault against such legislation on the state level. One by one, state legislatures repealed these laws, usually with little fanfare, justifying their actions by saying that the statutes were "unenforceable" or "unnecessary" or "probably unconstitutional", despite the fact that the Supreme Court has consistently upheld the right of states to pass and enforce antisodomy laws.

At last count only a minority of the states (twenty-four and the District of Columbia) still carried such statutes on the books. Yet it is important that our legal system reflect what we believe about matters that have perennially been regarded as moral. We have laws on the books outlawing rape and child molestation because we believe these things are wrong. We should likewise reaffirm our belief in the immorality of sodomy by putting antisodomy statutes back on the books in those states where they have been dropped.

Second, in reaffirming this belief, we will also be strength-
ening our commitment to the American family and its central
place in our society. The union of a man and woman in marriage is the single most important social institution in Western
civilization. Since Genesis and the *Odyssey*, tribes, cities,
states, and nations have been based on the bedrock of family.
A Greek child was called by his father's name in addition to a
given name. Rome was a city of families, each with its patri-
arch or *pater familias*, who spoke for the rest of his people in the
councils of the empire. The twelve tribes of Israel were
regarded as nothing more than extended families. And Chris-
tianity, with its emphasis on the Holy Family as a model for all
human conduct, has extended and broadened the meaning of
family to cosmic proportions.

Only in a modern ideological state like Nazi Germany or
Soviet Russia has the family unit been denigrated or replaced
in the interest of totalitarian regimentation. At least such has
been the case until very recently, when—for reasons that
should be obvious—homosexual activists have begun to attack
those ancient social arrangements, either charging that the
family has been the crucible of bigotry and intolerance or else
redefining the family to include cohabiting for sexual purposes
by members of the same sex. Homosexual organizations, bol-
stered by such allies as the National Organization of Women,
are demanding that (1) they be given the same tax breaks as
traditional families, (2) they be given equal consideration in
the adoption of children, (3) their sexual arrangements be
taught as valid "alternative life-styles" in public schools, and
(4) private institutions, such as businesses, give them the same
fringe benefits (insurance, bereavement leave, etc.) that they
offer to married people. Lesbians have even begun, through
artificial insemination, to give birth to their own children,
sometimes sharing them with the homosexual sperm donor,
as reported recently on PBS.

These demands endanger the very survival of the family as
we know it, and the only way to make certain that such recommendations are not put into practice is to reinstitute laws

against sodomy in all states. By so doing we would settle the question of rights and prerogatives now in dispute, saying emphatically that homosexuals per se have no rights other than those they enjoy by virtue of being citizens of the United States.

In passing such laws, we would also affirm a normative way of life for all Americans: that they are born and nurtured in traditional families where children have both mothers and fathers and hence learn to understand the marvelous union of man and woman that continually leads to the rebirth of life and love and hope on earth.

As we have seen in the case of AIDS, widespread homosexual behavior is a formidable threat to public health. The variety of things these people do exposes them to a range of infections that normal people do not encounter. For example, anal intercourse is unhealthy in more ways than one. In addition to exposing both partners to HIV infection, this unnatural behavior frequently spreads hepatitis B, a killing virus that is frequently found among homosexuals and that, like HIV, has polluted the bloodstream and caused the death of innocent transfusion recipients, including comedian Danny Kaye. Hepatitis B attacks the liver and can cause cirrhosis as well as other potentially fatal complications. It is so dangerous that most health care workers are routinely vaccinated against it. The general population, however, is at the mercy of the virus if exposed.

In addition to Hepatitis B, perhaps the second most deadly of the predominantly homosexual viruses, there are four diseases that cause what doctors originally called "gay bowel syndrome" (GBS): hepatitis A, amebiasis, shigellosis, and giardiasis. GBS is a complex of symptoms (fever, diarrhea, etc.) that first occurred in a number of California homosexuals and later spread throughout the country, eventually infecting heterosexuals as well. More like a convention of infections than a single disease, a GBS sufferer is often invaded by at least two of the organisms and sometimes all of them. Each of these diseases, however, is devastating. For example, amebiasis causes dysentery and liver abscesses, while giardiasis can result in painful and chronic inflammation of the intestinal tract. Shigellosis is often fatal in children. Like typhoid, gay bowel syndrome can be transmitted by the handling of food, a fact that makes it particularly threatening to the community at large, since, according to the *New England Journal of Medicine*, in a heavily populated area like San Francisco, 10 percent of those infected with amebiasis, giardiasis, and shigellosis in 1980 were working as food handlers.

As noted earlier, AIDS patients, almost three-fourths of whom are homosexuals, increasingly contract tuberculosis, a disease that is still a killer in the United States, despite the complacency of the public at large. TB can be transmitted by sneezing and coughing; and while in the past the infection rate has been extremely low, there is some concern among medical authorities that tuberculosis may be more infectious in conjunction with HIV.

Another disease that goes hand in hand with HIV is cytomegalovirus, or CMV. The incidence of CMV in AIDS patients is extremely high, close to 100 percent in some estimates; and while its symptoms are often negligible, it can damage unborn children. In fact, a nurse in California has charged that her son was born malformed because she contracted CMV while working with AIDS patients. She has also charged that the hospital where she worked refused to let her wear gloves and a mask out of concern for the feelings of the patients.

It is important to note that these diseases are contagious through casual contact, so the community at large is directly threatened with infection as the result of the way homosexuals conduct themselves. This fact suggests that what people do in the privacy of their own bedroom is indeed the business of the community at large—if it threatens the lives and health of other people. To argue otherwise is to strike at the very idea of society.

Of course, homosexuals are chiefly responsible for the rise of sexually transmitted diseases in recent years. Following

Thomas Parran's successful campaign in the 1930s and 1940s, syphilis was under control. But with the advent of the homosexual movement and the prodigious sexual license practiced in the bathhouses and elsewhere, infectious syphilis has risen precipitously in the last few years. A recent study conducted at one hospital showed that during a two-year period, over three times as many homosexual males were treated for syphilis as heterosexual males. As for gonorrhea, almost 44 percent of the male cases were homosexuals — though they make up a fraction of the total population. Other studies indicate the same obvious truth: homosexuals are the prime source of sexually transmitted diseases in this country.

It has only been with the legalization of this unhealthy behavior and the increased tolerance of the normal population that these various diseases have become problematic and even epidemic. We have done homosexuals themselves the greatest injustice by permitting such license, since they have become the chief victims of their own misbehavior. So for their sakes, as well as for the rest of the nation, we must reimpose the kind of restrictions that have kept this kind of behavior in check since the beginnings of the nation.

Finally, we must reinstate traditional prohibitions against homosexuality in order to establish a sense of order and decency in our society, to reconnect us with our normative past. The history of America, like the history of every great nation, is based on a sense of purpose that transcends mere growth and self-interest. In our finest moments we have thought of ourselves as the last and greatest frontier of Western civilization, as the founders of a City on the Hill where prosperity was not the end of our existence but merely the by-product of virtue. As long as we concentrated on being virtuous, we were also successful, and our power and influence seemed to grow naturally.

However, in the past twenty years we have undergone profound changes, and for the first time we have begun to renounce our own wisdom and virtue as a people. In fact, if you examined only our sexual conduct during this period, you would have to say we have changed more in one generation than we did in the first 175 years of our history. Such changes are bound to affect the way we will fare as a nation, not only in the next 175 years but more quickly, in the next two decades.

Let us take a look at what has happened to nations whose histories parallel our own, remembering that thus far, no society has outlived time.

The world is full of ruined monuments to the failure of civilization—or, to be more precise, the failures of numerous civilizations, each organized according to different principles, each brought to disaster in a different way. Some of them died slow deaths, stretching out over many centuries, like the Roman and the Chinese empires. Some were brought to sudden ruin, like Carthage. But in the greatest of civilizations, there is usually a common thread at the end, a corruption of spirit that leads to selfishness and preoccupation with pleasure, eventually to the exclusion of what is usual and normal. At that point, excess and perversion come into fashion, and after that—catastrophe. There are numerous examples of such decadence, and at the end of great civilizations you almost always find homosexuality—widespread, energetic, enormously proud of itself.

Some people are not sure whether Sodom and Gomorrah were real places, but I'm inclined to believe in the historical existence of at least Sodom. I wouldn't necessarily have said so twenty or even ten years ago, but San Francisco has persuaded me. No one doubts the existence of Rome, when the Emperor Nero was on the throne and Petronius, in his *Satyricon*, describes the wild sexual excesses of the court, with particular emphasis on the practice of sodomy, which he treats as an amusing sport.

When the Spaniards came to Mexico in the early sixteenth century, the Mayan civilization they found was no longer the healthy, vital culture that had produced so much wealth and learning. It too had become decadent and self-indulgent. The pleasure-obsessed upper classes were sacrificing human beings, engaging in orgies, and practicing sodomy without shame. The shocked Spaniards put the Mayan rulers to the sword.

By the seventeenth century, the once-powerful Venetian republic, one of the earliest European examples of representative democracy, had become worldly and sybaritic. Women were walking through the streets covered with jewels, their faces painted, their bare breasts exposed. Again homosexuality among men was widespread and unabashed, a symbol of the waste of sexual desire in a world that had lost all its meaning.[16]

Germany toward the end of the Weimar republic was a society of economic chaos and moral bankruptcy. Perhaps the best interpreter of its perversity was popular composer Kurt Weil, whose cabaret songs and ironic musical plays depicted the cynical self-indulgence in a world in which homosexual intrigues take the place of normal sexuality for many of the jaded characters. Weil's Germany (which he eventually fled) was the nation that Adolph Hitler took over only a few years later.

And now some people are saying that the United States of America has come to the same point in its history, when its religious and moral traditions are held in contempt by increasing numbers of its people, when a growing segment of the population regards life as meaningless except during moments of self-gratification, when promiscuous sexual behavior is everywhere, and when once again homosexuality is not only accepted but applauded.

Are we going to be destroyed like the great civilizations of the past, because we no longer have the moral will to resist corruption? I don't really believe so, though sometimes I am ready to concede defeat. As Billy Graham was quoted as saying, "If God doesn't destroy the United States of America, He owes Sodom and Gomorrah an apology."

[16] Judith Cressy, "Empire of Reflection", *Arts and Antiques* (January, 1988), 82.

V. The Rejection of Antidiscrimination Laws

Proposed AIDS antidiscrimination laws are popular these days because they make specious appeals to the best in Americans — their sense of fair play and their belief in tolerance. But these particular laws are not really designed to help the afflicted or serve the cause of a just society. Instead, they are wrongheaded attempts to force the community to accept homosexuality as a valid alternative to normal sexuality and to do so at the risk of the nation's health. At best they are irrational or inconsistent. At worst they are devious and perverse.

When the President's AIDS Commission, by a split vote (8 to 5), recommended antidiscrimination legislation, I wrote the following letter to the White House, in which I asked fifteen questions for which there are no easy answers. Of course, these questions were purely rhetorical. I didn't expect answers, only that the President's advisors consider each of them carefully before coming to any final conclusions.

Here are the questions:

1. The President's AIDS Commission recommended that it be made a crime for anyone with HIV to donate to the blood supply. How do we reconcile this particular prohibition with antidiscrimination laws? How can the operator of a blood bank refuse the offered blood of someone who is HIV positive when such a person would be able to claim that to refuse to take the blood is an act of discrimination?

2. Do we intend to say to the life insurance industry that life insurance must be written to an applicant who is HIV positive without giving companies power to adjust premiums appropriately? Science now tells us that the only cofactor for a person who is infected is time, and that the median is about seven years after infection until death. Are we prepared to coerce the life insurance industry into insuring, without realistic adjustments, HIV-infected applicants? Such a posture would, of course, bankrupt these businesses.

3. Do we intend to say to the health insurance industry that it may not discriminate against an HIV-infected applicant for

the same reasons as life insurers? The average health care costs for an AIDS patient have been estimated somewhere between $75,000 and $100,000. Unwise antidiscrimination laws would seemingly allow an applicant with no history of having procured health insurance to compel a health insurance carrier to write a full-coverage policy at the same rates as for the healthy the day after such a person learns of his HIV status. Are we prepared to discriminate against insured persons with diabetes, cancer, heart trouble, and the like who uniformly have their policies adjusted based on their afflictions? This will be the effect of antidiscrimination legislation.

4. Are we saying to America's work force that they are required to work side by side with HIV-infected persons even though 30 percent to 44 percent of the infected, who are otherwise asymptomatic, are manifesting dementia with a consequent impairment of motor functions? Are we willing to say to employees that their safety on the job may possibly be compromised as a result of antidiscrimination status for HIV-infected persons?

5. Are we saying to uninfected Americans that they must agree to work with HIV-infected individuals with infectious tuberculosis, transmitted through the respiratory system, and numerous other infectious opportunistic diseases because to discharge such individuals would be discriminatory? Are we asking Americans to consent to exposure to TB given the revealing evidence that in a New York study of public hospitals 42 percent of male TB patients between the ages of twenty-five and forty-four were also HIV positive?

6. Are we saying to the American people, particularly pregnant women, that they must consent to be exposed to cytomegalovirus (CMV), excreted by a person with ARC or AIDS and known to cause birth defects, because to fail to do so would be discriminatory? Are we saying that pregnant nurses will now be required to take care of AIDS patients, notwithstanding certain exposure to CMV?

7. Are we saying to health care workers in America that they may not wear gowns, masks, and gloves at their own dis-

cretion in taking care of AIDS patients? Do the sensitivities of a few patients override the obligation of health care workers to protect themselves from CMV, tuberculosis, and Epstein-Barr syndrome, a precursor to mononucleosis?

8. Are we saying to a church that has qualified for participation in the proposed federal child care program, thus establishing a federal nexus, that an applicant for a teaching position should be hired regardless of antibody status or regardless of the fact that he is a self-avowed homosexual or drug addict? Regardless of the fact that he might openly share his life-style with his students, notwithstanding that homosexuality and drug abuse are specifically proscribed by the religious beliefs of the church?

9. Are we saying that a theological seminary should be required to admit for theological training a self-avowed homosexual or drug addict who is HIV infected and who claims such status is his guarantee against discrimination? Would any church or synagogue in America with a vacancy for a pastor, priest, or rabbi be required to hire a self-avowed homosexual or drug addict who insists that his antibody status provides him an open door as a result of antidiscrimination laws?

10. Are we saying to our United States military that it now must enlist the infected? Are we saying that they now must admit a self-avowed homosexual into their ranks because the infected may not be discriminated against? Are we saying to our military authorities, who now routinely discharge homosexuals, that any among them who are HIV infected may not be discharged because of the adoption of this proposed antidiscrimination legislation?

11. Are we saying that persons with *curable* communicable diseases whose status is routinely reported to public health authorities, in confidence, will continue to be reported, but persons who are carriers of HIV, an *incurable* communicable disease, will not be reported? Are we willing to discriminate against the former to give special privilege to the latter?

12. Are we ready to say to the states of the Union that require a man and a woman to get a marriage license, that when two infected men apply for a marriage license, each showing proof of being HIV infected, that a state may not deny a marriage license to the men because of the antidiscrimination law being proposed?

13. Are we saying that a Boy Scout troop or Cub Scout den, looking for a male leader, would be required to hire a male homosexual who shows proof of HIV infection because this proposed antidiscrimination law precludes discrimination against someone who is infected?

14. Are we saying to the American people who, as lessors renting a home or apartment, or as employers wanting to hire workers, that the decision can no longer be founded on affirming the heterosexual ethic because antidiscrimination laws proscribe discrimination against someone infected, 73 percent of whom, nationally, are male homosexuals and 17 percent are IV drug users?

15. Are we saying that an infected homosexual has the right to teach his homosexual philosophy in a public school by virtue of his badge of HIV infection?

In addition to asking these questions, I would make the following point: the three cities in America with the largest proportion of AIDS—52 percent of all cases nationwide—are New York, San Francisco, and Los Angeles. All three have antidiscrimination laws.

Currently we are a divided nation—divided in our understanding of what to do about AIDS, divided in our attitudes toward the toleration of homosexuality, divided in our commitment to a traditional public morality. Such a division has not existed in America since the Civil War, and it will not be easily repaired. We have come to the moment, however, when we will have to decide which view of the future will prevail. In the next two to four years we will be forced by the further progress of this epidemic to commit ourselves irrevocably to one view or the other. Obviously, the choice we make will determine whether or not we survive as a people.

I am by no means certain what that choice will be. I believe that we have the moral will to restore traditional American morality, win the war against AIDS, and go on to create an even greater nation for our children and grandchildren. But I also think we have the capacity to make the wrong choice and plunge our people, and indeed the entire West, into a dark night of the soul that could last hundreds of years before the flame is again lit. It has happened before. It can happen again. It is in full knowledge of such a grim possibility that I have written this book.

INDEX

Abortion, 62-65, 157
About Your Sexuality, 161-69, 171-73, 175
Abt and Associates, 71-73
Acquired behavior theories, 45-56
Acquired Immune Deficiency Syndrome, *see* AIDS
Adamopoulas, D. A., 43
Adams, Terry, 70
Advocate, 103, 105, 124, 127-28
Affirmation—United Methodists for Gay and Lesbian Concerns, 100-101
AIDS: Sexual Behavior and Intravenous Drug Use, 150-51
AIDS, and antidiscrimination laws, 224-28; and contact tracing, 214-17; federal money for, 15-16; and homosexual deaths, 152-55; and the HRCF, 149; litigation, 75-87; medical policies for, 16; and public policy, 187-228; religious response to, 111-13; reporting, 211-14; and sex

education, 159-60, 178-80; and sodomy laws, 217-23; widespread testing for, 198-211
AIDS Coalition to Unleash Power (ACT-UP), 17
AIDS Commission, 224
Alabama, 76, 185, 211
Albert Einstein College of Medicine, 55
Alternate life-style, 131-32
Altman, Dennis, as homosexual activist, 49-50; on homosexual movement, 122-24; on the homosexual's identity, 141; on National Gay and Lesbian Task Force, 144; use of homosexual rhetoric by, 128
Amebiasis, 219-20
American Association of Sex Educators, Counselors, and Therapists (AASECT), 161-62
American Civil Liberties Union (ACLU), and AIDS epidemic, 154; and the hate crime bill, 71; and legal aid for homosexuals, 83-84; as political action group,